FASTER BETTER WINDSURFING

Faster Better Windsurfing

Uwe Preuss
Jochen Taaks
Sepp Winbeck

STANFORD MARITIME
LONDON

Stanford Maritime Limited
Member Company of the George Philip Group
12–14 Long Acre London WC2E 9LP
Editor Phoebe Mason

First published in Great Britain 1984
English edition © Stanford Maritime Ltd 1984

Translated into English by Barbara M. Snell

Originally published as *Schneller Besser Windsurfen*
Copyright © Buchheim Editions SA Fribourg 1984
and Mosaik Verlag GmbH, München

Set in 11/12 Monophoto Univers 689 by
Tameside Filmsetting Limited
Ashton-under-Lyne, Lancashire

Printed in Switzerland by
Zobrist & Hof AG, 4410 Liestal

British Library Cataloguing in Publication Data
Preuss, Uwe
  Faster, Better Windsurfing.
  1. Windsurfing
  I. Title   II. Taaks, Jochen
  III. Winbeck, Sepp   IV. Schneller, Besser
  Windsurfen. *English*
  797.1'24   GV811.63.W56   .

ISBN 0-540-07284-2

Contents

Introduction

With *Faster, Better Windsurfing* we have endeavoured to write a straightforward guide for the first steps to this sport, at the same time offering the more experienced sailor advice on developing his skills. We not only want to help you increase your sailing speed: our primary aim is to introduce you as rapidly as possible to modern windsurfing enabling you to master a wider range of techniques in greater safety, and above all achieve increased enjoyment.

This book has not only been written for old hands looking for new stimulus from windsurfing; the newcomer to the sport will also find the answers to his questions and be able to follow descriptions of trouble-free techniques for starting from scratch. Both the novice and the more experienced windsurfer, including those who learned according to outdated methods and are out of practice, will find that this book contains all the basic principles set out concisely for easy reference.

Within the covers of this small book we have not been able to give you all the possibilities offered by windsurfing, but from our own experience we know that all skills are based on the mastery of basic key principles. Greater enjoyment and achievement can then be gained simply from learning a new technique or trick. We have therefore placed particular emphasis on clear and detailed descriptions of these key principles.

In addition to the pure fun of the sport we must not forget that the windsurfer is responsible for a vessel. He is a sailor who must know and obey the rules, regulations and codes of behaviour applicable to everyone. He must avoid endangering not only himself but causing a nuisance to others practising water sports or engaged in commercial transport. A number of local authorities regard windsurfing with a certain suspicion; there is talk of banning it from some areas and imposing limitations on others. Our sport would be the poorer for being confined to restricted zones.

When considerate behaviour, awareness of the natural conditions on which our sport depends and good board control are automatically observed by all windsurfers there will be less talk of imposing restrictive measures.

This book can do much to contribute to the provision of the greater knowledge which we feel is so vital for the continued popularity of the sport. The greater skill in controlling the board depends on you alone, but the practical side of this book contains useful information to help you to achieve this. The more you use these hints to improve your ability the quicker you will obtain results. If you want to be able to sail your board faster and better we recommend you to take a course from an experienced and qualified instructor at an appropriate windsurfing school.

Rigging the Board

You will no doubt be able to rig your sailboard without these instructions, and many manufacturers go in for special features which we cannot cover here. However, we suggest that you compare our suggested routine with your own and adopt any ideas you may consider helpful.

You will not need to be convinced of the importance of taking care over rigging your board. A correctly rigged sailboard will be able to manoeuvre better and faster, and reduces the liklihood of an accident due to faulty equipment.

If you are not familiar with the knots used in rigging the sail please refer to pages 66–9.

Assembling the mast, mast foot fitting and the sail

Lay the head of the sail out on the downwind side and slide the mast into the luff sleeve. Before putting the heel fitting on the mast make sure that it is clean of sand by feeling round inside the heel with your fingers, as shown. You should of course have already shaken any sand out of the mast: if

sand trickles down it will wear the heel into a taper. You can apply Vaseline or a similar grease which will always ensure easy removal of the mast from the heel fitting. Attach the downhaul line for the lower corner of the sail to

Before stepping the mast make sure it is clean inside to prevent sticking and jamming.

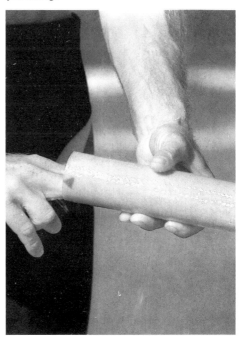

the mast heel fitting and make a bowline just above and as close to it as you can with the loose end. Now pass the downhaul twice through the eye in the tack of the sail and the bowline. Tie it temporarily with two half-hitches above the bowline; the downhaul has yet to be tightened finally. The resulting block-and-tackle effect will reduce the force needed to set up the downhaul and enable you to pull the sail down easily.

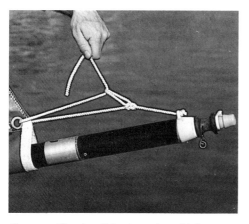

For an effective 'block and tackle' arrangement for tensioning the downhaul, tie a bowline close to the mast foot.

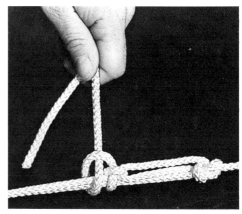

Having taken the line through the tack and the bowline and tightened it, secure it with two half-hitches.

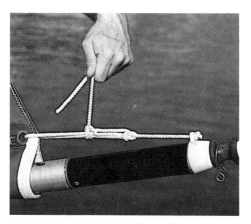

The finished method of attaching the downhaul with a bowline and two half-hitches. Make free end fast.

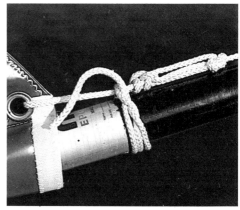

Secure the free end of the downhaul with sufficient half-hitches round the mast to keep it up off the board as you might catch your foot in it.

Attaching the boom to the mast

Lash the boom end fitting to the mast with a mast hitch at about eye level. If you expect to be sailing in a strong breeze and have a planing board you may wish to set the boom higher, but remember that manoeuvring is more difficult with a very high boom (especially the water start: see page 52). You should leave a space of at least 10 cm (4 in) between the hitch and the top of the notch in the sail, as the luff sleeve will pull down a little when the sail is set up hard with the

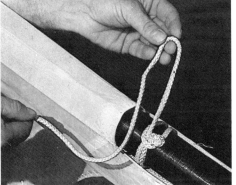

Fig. 1: *The mast hitch*

downhaul. Pull the free end of the inhaul line through one of the holes in the boom end fitting, take it round the mast, through another hole and into the cleat. Now you can take up the slack on the inhaul and bring the boom end quite close in against the mast before pushing the free end of the line into the teeth of the jam cleat and finishing off with two half-hitches round the boom.

Figs. 2–4: *Securing the boom to the mast*

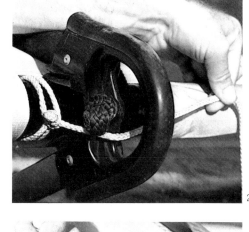

Inserting the sail battens

One end of the batten usually has slight notches and is held in place in the sail with elastic. Push the battens into the pockets as far as they will go and slip the other end under the flap on the leech. The elastic presses the batten into this pocket so that it is held in the sail. (See page 15 for batten tension and sail setting.)

Tighten the sail with the outhaul

Secure the clew outhaul line with a bowline in the end through the wishbone end fitting. Thread the loose end of the line through the eye in the clew of the sail, back through the end fitting and once again through the eye in the clew. This gives an effective and simple mechanical advantage.

We recommend the following easy and effective method of tightening the outhaul (below). Lay the mast down across the wind with the clew of the sail downwind. Set the sail by tightening your outhaul line until it is the right shape. Then pinch the outhaul line where it runs through the eye in the clew tightly between your thumb and forefinger, make the first half-hitch round the outhaul a slipknot and pull it hard. Secure the line with a second half-hitch in the loop once you have tensioned the sail to your satisfaction. Your sail is now rigged, but its final setting is still to come. The tail of the outhaul is tied round the boom in a clove hitch.

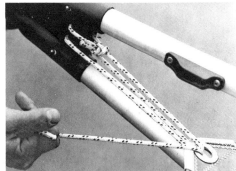

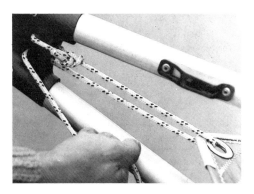

Setting the Sail

Having set the sail turn the rig to the wind to see if there are any wrinkles or creases which will affect its action. Start by spilling the wind out of the sail and then hauling it in slowly. By looking at the shape of the seams running across the sail you can see whether the greatest fullness or curvature is in the right place. A full sail should not touch the leeward side of the wishbone. If you are not sure whether the wishbone is right for the mast, you can check by looking at it: if the mast is too stiff for your sail the greatest curvature will not be in the correct place, which is in the second quarter of the full chord length (the line from mast to clew) of the sail. If the mast is too stiff there will be a short belly in the cloth just behind the luff sleeve: you will not be able to cure this by adjusting the tension or trimming the sail and it will constantly spill wind. But if the mast is not sufficiently stiff it will also affect the shape of the sail: the curvature will be fuller than was intended by its design and the sailcloth will go into marked wrinkles radiating from the luff to the clew, turning your costly canvas into an ineffective, below-average sail. If the profile of the sail is as bad as this, no amount of trimming will counteract it.

We have set out on the next page the reasons for creases and ways of eliminating them.

Jürgen Hönscheid with a well set sail

Hints on Sail Setting

Vertical creases or wrinkles from the masthead to the tack
● Mast too stiff
—Use a more flexible mast
● Downhaul set up too tight
—Loosen downhaul
● Outhaul not tight enough
—Tighten outhaul

Horizontal creases along the luff close to the mast
● Downhaul not tight enough
—If the luff sleeve is made of nylon wet it before trimming the sail, then tighten the downhaul.

Large horizontal creases radiating from the clew to the mast
● Mast not stiff enough
—Use a stiffer mast
● Outhaul set too tight
—Let out the outhaul a little

Large creases radiating from the tack
● Downhaul set too tight
—Ease it off

We would like to mention here some features which are peculiar to modern sail cutting.

Powerhead or fathead sails have at least one batten which reaches right across to the mast. This batten should not be inserted until the sail has been set. If you try to insert the batten beforehand it will either be impossible or you will damage the pocket and the sail. These battens are usually stronger and thicker at one end as they not only reinforce the leech but also give the sail its profile: the thinner end should be inserted first into the batten pocket. The battens are usually held in place and under tension on the leech with Velcro tape. Horizontal wrinkles around these full-width battens indicate too little tension. Do not let the Velcro get dirty or it will cease to be effective and the batten may slip out. Many sails are provided with a leech-line sewn into the leech, which can be adjusted for tension at the clew. Do not overtighten this line: it is only there to remove fluttering of the leech and cannot correct a badly set sail. If there is too much tension on the leechline you will have a hooked, i.e. turned over, leech which will adversely affect the separation of the airflow at the edge of the sail.

▲ *Not enough downhaul tension and the outhaul too tight*

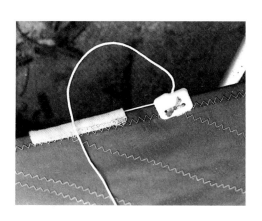

Many people find that they have horizontal creases along the foot of the sail, running from the tack to the clew, which no amount of tension adjustment will remove. These folds are not usually the result of poor setting of the sail but are caused by its construction. The foot of the sail should have a hook in the edge to reduce pressure equalization between the leeward and windward airflow which inhibits forward thrust. This effect can also be produced by a rolled foot: part of the fold will go of its own accord when the sail is correctly loaded by a strong wind.

Not enough tension on the top batten: the mast may be too stiff for the sail

Equipment Checklist

When you have finished rigging the board check the following:

The Rig
- *Replace frayed or worn ropes.*
- *Does the heel of the mast rotate freely?*
  If not, unstep the mast and clean it.
- *Is there a gap between the boom end fitting and the mast?*
  If so, slacken the outhaul and re-tighten the inhaul.
- *Are there any visible cracks in the boom fittings? If so, replace.*
- *Does the mast hitch touch the sail?*
  If so, slacken the outhaul and
  downhaul, loosen the mast hitch and push it up or down.
- *Are the batten packets and end fastenings sound?*
  If not, restitch or replace them.

The Board
- *Is the surface of the board slippery?*
  If so, wash clean and apply wax.
- *Is the skin of the board damaged?*
  If so, repair small holes or cracks; larger damaged areas must be treated by an expert. Tape over any damage temporarily, to keep water out.
- *Can the daggerboard and mast foot be easily moved and adjusted?*
  If not, clean the fittings.
- *Are the fins firm? If not, tighten the screws or replace them.*

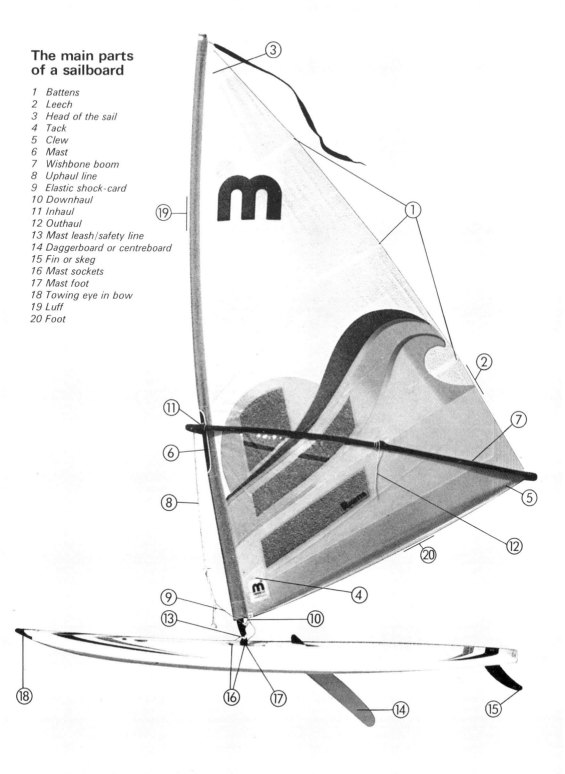

The main parts
of a sailboard

1 Battens
2 Leech
3 Head of the sail
4 Tack
5 Clew
6 Mast
7 Wishbone boom
8 Uphaul line
9 Elastic shock-card
10 Downhaul
11 Inhaul
12 Outhaul
13 Mast leash/safety line
14 Daggerboard or centreboard
15 Fin or skeg
16 Mast sockets
17 Mast foot
18 Towing eye in bow
19 Luff
20 Foot

Balancing or Trimming the Board

Board trim is effected by the position of the foot of the mast on the board; the position, size and pivoting system of the centreboard or daggerboard; and the number, size, shape and position of the fins or skegs. These can be combined in an almost limitless number of ways: also, they act differently on every board shape and we have certainly not yet reached the limits of design evolution and development. At this stage, therefore, we will only discuss the position of the mast step and the number and position of the fins. There are three different arrangements of fins on funboards which can affect the performance markedly.

Single fin. One (large) fin holds the board on course. Single fins, especially straight, raked-back ones, make for greatest speed, but sailing with a single fin carries a degree of risk as if you lose your fin you will have to paddle.

Twin fins. Two medium sized fins placed side by side are safer than a single one. The board will not be quite so fast but it will sail closer to the wind and one broken fin will not leave you in such difficulty. Twin fins are better for manoeuvres such as sharp turns, as one of them will stay in the water.

Thrusters. Two small fins at the sides and ahead of a medium sized main fin have proved to be a good combination for sailing in waves, especially for small boards. Thruster fins curved on one side have been taken from surfboards. Their advantage is also disputed among surfriders, however, since they reduce speed. They only provide good manoeuvrability if toed-in towards the centreline of the board: otherwise they have the reverse effect. They are not suitable when manoeuvrability as well as speed is important.

Typical arrangement of thrusters on a funboard

Mast tracks

Most boards are provided with two mast sockets as standard. They should be at least 15 cm (6 in) apart to perform any useful function. Sailing with the mast in the back socket reduces the planing surface, makes the board faster and more manoeuvrable. The front socket is useful when sailing close to the wind, helps a funboard to sail in a falling wind and makes the board easier to plane, but your ability to turn is reduced. The fact that the forward position is best suited to sailing closehauled and the aft one is better for sailing on a broad reach encouraged enterprising perfectionists to look at the idea of fitting a sliding fitting on a track to vary the position of the mast foot.

While in theory being able to achieve the ideal sail balance is fine, in practice efforts to mass-produce a satisfactory fitting of this type have not been successful. The main difficulties are the lateral force on the heel of the mast and the need for an adjustable but at the same time quick-release device, which above all must be durable and not liable to clog up and jam. If you think you can overcome these problems, try a mast track. To date, experience has shown that moving the mast while underway cannot be accomplished very quickly and easily.

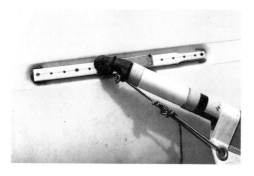

Mast track on a Pan Am board: the movable slide is released by a foot-operated catch

Carrying the Board and Rig to the Water

After carefully checking your preparations carry the board and rig down to the water separately, although this is not recommended if waves are breaking on the shore or if the wind is so strong that the fully rigged sail could take off on its own without the board to hold it down.

Carrying the rig

Always carry the rig with the mast leading and at right angles to the wind and the wishbone downwind, and always lay it down in this position. Some people like to carry it across their body and others above their head (see page 21). In very strong or gusty winds, or if you are inexperienced, lift and carry the rig as follows. Take hold of the wishbone from above with one hand and grip the mast with the other just above the wishbone. Lift the rig and let the wind help support it. You will now find that you have to walk backwards into the wind!

There are two methods of avoiding this. You can either carry the sail and mast above your head while holding the wishbone from underneath with the other hand. In this way you can carry the sail forwards into the wind with greater comfort and it is also easier to negotiate any obstacles in the way. Or if the rig is too heavy to carry this way you can support the sail on your head while controlling it with the mast and wishbone. When you reach the water's edge, if there is nothing in the way you can put the sail down by 'throwing' it forward into the wind, saving yourself a few steps.

Carrying the board

Now you must bring the board to the water with its daggerboard and fin in position. Always carry the board in the way shown in the photo. Take a firm hold of the mast step, inserting two fingers of one hand in the mast well, and hold the centreboard with the other hand. It can be very tiring to carry a board on your own if there is much wind as it may catch either the bow or stern and throw you off balance. In a strong wind it is better for two people to carry a board.

If possible, fit the rig to the board in knee-deep water. Do not forget to fasten the retaining line which keeps the rig attached to the board.

Getting out of the water

To leave the water, reverse the above routine. Undo the retaining line and unstep the mast, drop the rig into the water and pull the board ashore to a safe place. Fetch the rig and put it where it will not be in anyone's way. As soon as you have removed the rig loosen the outhaul and the downhaul to take the tension off the sail. If the wind is fresh the rig must be laid to leeward of other people, and you may need someone else to help you by holding the mast. Do not let the sail flap in the wind or you will soon ruin the best sailcloth.

▲ *Normal width funboards can be carried under an arm with the top of the board towards you.*

▼ *Carrying the sail in front of you at waist height or above your head, with the mast to windward.*

Hauling up the Sail

Until you have mastered the water start, or if wind conditions are inadequate, you will have to pull the sail up out of the water with the uphaul. Everyone who has had some experience of sailing in a strong wind knows that pulling up the rig again and again is more tiring than the actual sailing itself. With a suitable rig and the right technique this basic action can be rendered less strenuous.

The rig will demand less strength if
● you have a small sail and short wishbone
● the uphaul line reaches down to the board, and if it is a good thick rope with the shockcord attached about half a meter (2 ft) above the end knot.

Your technique will save your energy and your back if you
● keep your back straight and use your body weight to raise the sail
● let the wind help you to lift up the sail.

The basic uphauling technique requires the sail to be lying in the water to leeward of the board. Raising the sail when it is lying to windward is shown on page 24.

The Basic Technique
● *Stand with the feet equally spaced on either side of the mast*
Your feet, placed on the centre of the board, should point in the same direction to leeward as the mast with the weight evenly divided between them.

● *Starting position*
Take hold of the uphaul at the end knot, bend your knees slightly keeping your back straight. The mast may not be quite at right angles to the board (although this is the most stable position). It is more important that your toes are pointing exactly in line with the mast.

● *Raise the rig*
Lean back gently and try to use your weight as you straighten your legs. Keeping back and arms straight, pull either the mast or the clew in the direction of the stern, depending on which way the sail is lying. You have now lifted the rig so that the water can run out of the sleeve and off the sail. While raising the sail allow a little time for the board to turn round and point into the wind.

● *Pull the rig right up out of the water*
Even if the wind is only light, it will reward your patience by catching the luff and helping as you haul the sail hand-over-hand completely out of the water.

● *Catch hold of the mast and take up your basic position*
Take hold of the mast with one hand. The end of the wishbone should no longer touch the water. Stand with relaxed knees, keep your eyes up and hold the sail at right angles to the board. You are now standing in the basic position.

Pulling the sail up by using one's body weight. Hold the uphaul with one hand and wait until the water runs off the sail and out of the sleeve, before pulling it up. ▶

▲ The feet spaced equally in front and behind the mast (basic position).

In the basic position with the clew close to the water.　　　　　　　▶

Pulling up the sail from the windward side

You will not have been windsurfing for long before you find after scrambling back onto your board that your sail is lying to windward. There are two methods of bringing your sail round from the windward to the leeward side without exerting a great deal of strength:

● Pull the sail out of the water and let the wind blow it across to leeward, taking note which way it will blow. Half turn the board to leeward, moving round the sail. It is important to pull the clew out of the water quickly: either hold the uphaul very short or grab the mast itself to prevent the sail from touching the water on the leeward side, pulling it out of your hands.

● Pull the uphaul in the direction of the line of the mast, towards the bows or stern depending how the sail is lying (see page 25). The wishbone must be lying well across the board. Wait for the wind to bring either the bows or the stern round, making sure all the time that your feet remain pointing towards the top of the mast. As soon as the board is headed into the wind let the wind get under the sail and help you to pull it completely out of the water. As your board is already heading into the wind, you can decide whether to continue in the same direction or change your heading.

Hauling the sail up from the windward side without changing board direction, by letting it blow across.

Raising the sail by pulling the boom over the stern. When the bow is into the wind the sail can be hauled up.

Half Turn

For the beginner, the half turn is the simplest and safest method of changing the side that the sail is on in a small space. Take up the basic position, holding the mast (not the boom), lean the sail into the wind and let it turn the board in the required direction.

You should remember three points when carrying out a half turn:

- Hold your arms so that the end of the wishbone is just clear of the water. This will give you the fastest turning speed.
- While turning your feet should always point towards the end of the wishbone.
- Guide the rig only with the hand on the side to which you are leaning it.

In a confined space even the most experienced sailors will use a similar technique to bring their boards round.

The turn can be speeded up by holding the wishbone with the hand on the side to which the sail is leaning and the mast with the other. Place one foot in front of the mast and the other well behind it. You are now able to turn faster by applying greater force to the sail.

Apart from getting your board out of a tight spot, this turn will bring the wind abeam, from which position you can start sailing.

Turning the board by leaning the sail against the wind. Always hold the mast with the hand on the side towards which you are moving the sail.

Starting Sailing

By now you will have realized that there are certain basic differences between starting to move off as carried out by a novice and by the experienced windsurfer. The beginner prepares for his start carefully, positioning the board exactly, monitoring the angle of inclination of the rig, checking his foot positions and taking a good look around to make sure nothing is in the way.

As practised by the old hand, the transition from standing still to getting underway will be a continuous movement. He will move off from practically any point of sailing (angle to the wind), and can stop and start any time.

We describe below a precise starting routine for beginners so that you can learn *the key positions*.

The start position

Basic Position Place your feet in the centre of the board, evenly spaced on either side of the mast. Standing with relaxed knees, hold the sail at right angles to the board. You can maintain this position while looking around and taking your bearings.

This right-angle position, which must also be adhered to in the *start position*, determines the wind abeam heading which is the one from which you will start sailing in this method.

The Start Position Hold the mast only with the mast hand. Both feet should be behind the mast and pointing diagonally forwards; your arms should be fully extended to allow the board to keep at 90° to the wind.

The illustrations on pages 27–8 show the preparation and start in stages. These apply equally to both learners and experienced windsurfers.

● Pull the sail to windward by turning your body, continue until the rig is balanced and light to hold. Looking through the window in the sail past the bows you will be able to see whether the board is still lying with the wind abeam. Take a bearing on a landmark ahead which will keep you on your wind abeam course.

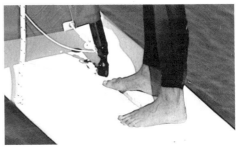

Feet in the start position

- Place your sail hand lightly on the boom. Keep your thumbs on top alongside your fingers and grasp the boom just in front of your shoulder. Whatever you do, do not pull with the sail hand or you won't be able to move the mast hand to the boom.
- Place your mast hand on the boom and both hands should now be level with your shoulders, at right angles to the board. The sail is still spilling the wind.
- By turning your shoulders back pull in the sail until it just holds the wind. You can now look ahead past the mast at your mark and depending on the power in the sail, lean back slightly putting your weight on your back foot. Your arms should remain bent with the elbows pointing

An experienced sailor in the waiting position ready to sail away immediately.

downwards.

With both hands on the wishbone turn your body round to one side then the other.

Turning your body round to the front will ease off the sail and lose way. This is the *waiting* or *holding position*.

Turning your body back hauls in the sail and starts you moving: it is the *sailing position*.

The Waiting or Holding Position is used by the expert to take a bearing and ascertain that his course is clear, to check how far he is from the shore and whether he has to take account of any current. If he has pulled the rig far enough over to windward before pulling in the sail he will be able to move off on any course, except running before the wind. We repeat: once the beginner can maintain the waiting or holding position steadily and without difficulty, he will be able to change course as he wishes, or return quickly to the basic start position; he will have mastered two key stages of learning and will be on the way to becoming a real windsurfer.

Starting in a Strong Wind

The strong wind start differs from the 'standard' start only in that the body weight is brought into play immediately. The sail must also be pulled in right away so that the relative wind which is produced by the increased speed of the board does not fill the wrong part of the sail.

In other respects the technique is the same as the standard start, but with the feet farther from the mast and the rig inclined more backwards and to windward.

Rotating the upper body backwards will cause the sailor to unbalance, throwing his weight to the windward side. In stronger winds your arms should be extended and your front leg will give you support from the front while by bending your back knee you can tension and position the sail. Bending the knee eases off and extending your leg hardens in the sail.

Quick Stop

Being able to stop quickly is part of the practised windsurfer's range of skills. This method of stopping the board as quickly as possible is only effective if you are sailing at an angle to the wind between closehauled and reaching. But as these are the most likely headings that you will be on, especially at first, mastering this emergency stop will bring your board simply and quickly to a standstill.

From the very first day on your board you will be able to drop the rig into the water, but this requires more space than a clean stop and leaves you unable to manoeuvre. Many crowded waters require constant avoiding action and a sail in the water may well cause a collision.

When making the emergency stop turn your body to 'back' the sail against the wind, holding the rig as far away from you as possible. You will need a little practice until you can lean all your weight against the sail without falling in. Try it out carefully at first until you find the position at which you must push to stop the board effectively without losing your balance.

If you find you cannot sail ahead after stopping, you will need to learn the *stop gybe*.

After stopping, continue to back the sail. If you drop the clew as far as you can your board will turn nearly in its own length.

Backing the sail by turning and pushing forwards with the upper body and pushing the rig into the wind.

Steering

Your sailboard is steered by a combination of tilting the rig in line with the chord of the sail and weighting the board so it tilts around its longitudinal axis together with loading the stern.

Steering with the rig

The most important prerequisite for clean steering is to have the appropriate rig position for the different points of sailing (see page 81).

- To luff up into the wind, tilt the rig to leeward along the direction of the sail's chord line.

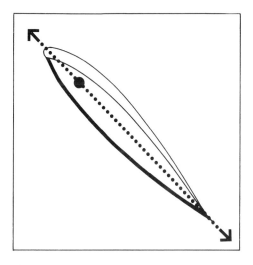

- To bear away, tilt the rig to windward along the direction of the sail's chord line.

Leave the sail in this position until the board has changed direction, then gradually change your stance to suit the new heading. It does not matter whether your weight is on your front or back foot.

The following tips will help you to improve your steering control:

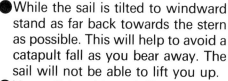

- While the sail is tilted to windward stand as far back towards the stern as possible. This will help to avoid a catapult fall as you bear away. The sail will not be able to lift you up.
- You will be able to luff up into the wind more quickly if you let some of the wind spill out of the sail. If you want to head up into the wind in order to come about quickly, let the mast hang out to leeward allowing the wind to fill the sail while remaining closehauled.

Luffing and bearing away are produced by tilting the rig back and to leeward or to windward.

Bearing away by weighting the wind-ward edge of a board with daggerboard.

Bearing away by weighting the leeward edge of a board without daggerboard.

Steering with the board

Depending on the type of board and the wind and wave conditions, tilting the board (foot steering) provides a supplementary or even a substitute method of steering control.

Boards with the centreboard extended can be steered by weighting the outside edge as you sail round a curve. To bear away put your weight on the windward edge of the board, and to head up into the wind transfer your weight to the leeward edge. The farther aft the load is on the side of the board, the greater will be the effect of this weight shift. You can try this out easily when running before the wind: the nearer the stern you stand when shifting your weight from one edge to the other the more effective it will be in changing your direction. A further factor is the size of the centreboard, and if it is a retractable one also its position. The nearer to the vertical the centreboard is, the greater will be the

turning reaction of the sailboard to lateral pressure.

Unsatisfactory results occur if the centreboard is small in proportion to the fin: there will be a lack of torque and the board will not respond to weighting. Foot steering will be ineffective and it will simply continue on its way. (This often happens with storm daggerboards which are angled backwards.)

Boards without centreboards are steered with the feet on the *inside* of the curve. In this case steering is affected by the shape of the stern, the size of the fins, and above all by the speed through the water. It is very simple to sail tight curves with this method of steering because the load on the inside of the curve and the necessary shift of the body weight to the inside make a natural and logical combined movement.

When you first try steering from the inside edge of the board:

● Only on a very small and fast board will you be able to forget about steering with the rig. If when you are bearing off you find you are taking the rig with you in the curve, the effect may be to counteract the effects of steering both with your weight and with the rig: your nice curve will turn into a straight line! So always remember to move the rig along the plane of the chord of the sail.

● Due to your weight on the edge of the board, inside position of your body at first is a reaction to the curve which the board follows, so do not throw your weight immediately to the inside when you want to sail in a curve. Only transfer enough body weight to prevent the centrifugal force from throwing you off balance and off the board.

Exercises

● In light wind practice tilting the rig exactly along the chord line, keeping feet and hands together.

● Steer the board with both feet in front of the foot of the mast.

● Steer the board with both feet behind the centreboard slot.

Jürgen Hönscheid in a 360° turn, one of the most radical manoeuvres on a funboard. Maximum use must be made of the leeward edge to perform this movement successfully.

Tacking

These two pages show the individual stages of a tack as it should be performed. The outer (bottom) sequence depicts a basic tack, the beginner's method; while the inner pictures show the quick tack as practised by an experienced sailor.

The beginner's method

The first concern of the novice is to change over the sail confidently from one side of the board to the other. To do this he will have to luff up, step quickly round the mast and continue the turn by leaning the sail against the wind until he can sail on the new tack. (See the half turn, page 26.)

● Luff up until you are sailing close to the wind, shift the mast hand and place one foot in front of the mast
● Luff up into the wind, let go your sail hand and step round in front of the mast
● Change mast hands
● Continue turning through the wind by leaning the sail against the wind until the basic position is reached
● Start off again on a beam reach.

Fast tacking

There are two objectives:

● To change the sail over from one side of the board to the other fast and smoothly;
● To gain as much ground into the wind as possible.

You can only achieve these two aims if:

● You luff up carefully with the correct sail position, and
● You start changing the sail over to the other side at just the right moment and continue the action dynamically, leaving the sail empty for the shortest possible time.

The sequence of quick tacking is:

● Luff up until the board has turned through the wind. Keep the mast hand on the mast, place the front foot in front of the mast, put weight on the back foot and let the rig hang out to leeward once you are on the wind.

Luffing up into the wind with the mast hand on the mast.

With the sail hand on the mast, release the old mast hand while holding the mast close to the body.

Pull the rig to windward with the new mast hand and start sailing again immediately.

When sailing closehauled keep the front foot just ahead of the mast.

Turn on the ball of the front foot and bring the back foot up to it

Continue turning on the ball of the old back foot and step towards the stern

- Remove the sail hand from the boom and transfer it to the mast. Take your weight off your back foot and bring it up by the front foot.
- Take a half turn with your front foot to the other side of the mast. Push the rig to windward to back the sail and bring your foot round behind the mast.
- Place your new sail hand on the boom.
- Haul in and start on your new reach.
- Ease off slightly so that you can bring the new mast hand onto the boom.

Backing the sail after coming about on a small board

This tack is also possible on small boards of 100L or less. Your mast foot must stay back as long as possible. If the bow digs in while changing sides, the sail must be pulled back far enough so that the bow comes back up.

Tacking Upwind

You will have learned already in your first lessons how to sail to windward.

The technique of beating – gaining ground against the wind by sailing close to the wind alternately on one tack and then on the other – is full of pitfalls, even for the experts. When sailing close to the wind its force works in the least favourable way: it produces maximum sideways thrust compared with its forward propulsion.

It is difficult to gauge the force of an offshore wind, and even the first tack made when reaching with the wind abeam will not tell you for certain. Only when you have made a trial tack back towards the shore will you have a good idea of the conditions for your return. The more closely you sail into the wind, the stronger it will become.

The best course to sail and the route you should take when tacking will vary from one board to another, depending on its lateral surface area and the shape and size of the sail. You will therefore have to find out for yourself how your board behaves when closehauled.

● Sail to make maximum speed to windward while going as close into the wind as possible to reach your windward destination. If your board has a large lateral surface area you should sail as close to the wind as you can. Even if you do not seem to be making much headway, your board will be making good speed to windward as its design does not give it too much leeway. If your board has a small lateral area, sail only as close to the wind as you can continue to make good speed through the water. These boards will make up windward distance by their greater speed on flatter tacks into the wind. If you 'pinch' or push your board too close into the wind the increasing leeway will cause you to lose ground to windward, and eventually your water speed will also drop. Only by comparing your performance against other boards will you have an idea as to how well your board performs closehauled.

● When the wind is steady you should make as few tacks as you can, for you lose speed and precious seconds every time you come about.

● When the wind frees (shifts aft) you should luff up into it. When the wind heads (comes more from the front) bear away a little. If the wind draws sharply ahead you should go about immediately as the other tack will get you to your destination faster. If you are heading for a particular point such as a buoy, come about for the last time when it lies exactly on your beam (it will be directly behind you).

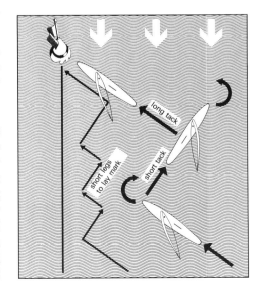

●If when tacking your destination is not directly to windward, you should alternate a slant or long tack (the side on which you head directly towards your goal) with a fetching or short tack on which you gain the necessary forward ground to make the next long tack. In order to make efficient progress when tacking, the long tack must always be closer to the wind than the short one.

Effective beating requires a great deal of experience and sensitivity to the slightest change in wind direction.

The first heat of a World Cup race. Pascal Matka, Philip Pudenz and Robby Naish are fighting for the lead.

Gybing

On these two pages we demonstrate a gybe with the daggerboard down, made by bringing the sail across with the wind behind.

The beginner's gybe Using this method, you steer the board round with the rig and the sail changes side when the wind is almost astern. You achieve this by leaning the rig against the wind as if you were carrying out a half turn until the board is on the new course with the wind again abeam.

● Check that the coast is clear to leeward
● Bear away by raking the rig until the wind is astern

● Bring your back foot forward and shift your front foot back slightly
● Hold the mast with your sail hand and release the mast hand
● Turn the board onto the new reach by leaning the sail against the wind
● The clew will nearly touch the water
● Start to sail on your new wind course with the wind abeam.

▲ **The advanced gybe:** *rig control is backed up and accelerated by weighting the stern and windward edge. The sail does not come across until the board is on its new tack.*

▼ **The beginner's gybe:** *bearing away follows from rig control alone. When the wind is astern the sail changes side as the rig is leant against the wind. Shift feet for the new heading when the wind is astern.*

3   2   1

The quick gybe with daggerboard

Keep two objectives in mind:
- A quick and safe sail changeover
- Minimum loss of momentum.

These aims can only be achieved if:
- Turning away from the wind is helped by weighting the outside of the board and the stern. You should therefore change the position of your feet as you begin to bear away.
- The sail remains at the best possible angle to the wind; and also when the clew is in a forward position it continues to provide forward thrust and acts as an aid to steering.

Sequence of the quick gybe with daggerboard:
- Check for room to leeward
- Place your front foot farther back and towards the windward side
- Bear away by shifting your weight onto your back foot and tilting the rig to windward
- Continue to bear away through the wind astern position until you have the wind abeam on the new side with the clew forward
- Slide your mast hand along the wishbone up to the mast

- Grasp the mast with your sail hand and swing the rig round
- As the sail swings, pull the rig hard to leeward with the new mast hand
- Place your sail hand on the boom and sail on your new course
- Ease off so that you can bring your mast hand onto the boom.

▲ *Mast hand slides along boom to mast before sail comes round.*

◄ *Strong weighting of stern and edge*

▼ *Steering is controlled by rig position and board angle.*

Gybing without the daggerboard

Boards without a daggerboard are steered by weighting the inside edge. You should already have achieved a certain degree of competence in this exhilarating technique before you attempt what is known as a *power gybe*. There are, however, two intermediate kinds of gybe without a daggerboard. In a moderate wind, if you are not sailing very fast you will need sufficient sail power throughout the entire manoeuvre to maintain planing speed and board control while tilting it with your weight.

The photo sequence on the next pages shows these ways of gybing.

A faster form of gybe has been developed for small boards, the *one-handed gybe* carried out without the power of the sail: it can be done only with a high degree of board control.

But first we will look at the classic power gybe.

Perfect example of board tilt and rig angle in an inside edge gybe

The classic power gybe shown in stages:
- Check for room to leeward
- Put your weight on the inside edge, by pressing down on your knee on the inside of the turn, and rake the rig to windward
- Bear away through the wind until it is abeam and the sail clew is pointing forward
- Change the position of your feet
- Slide your mast hand along the wishbone up to the mast
- Bring the sail round and continue sailing as described for the quick gybe (page 42).

Faults and tips

There are three faults which can spoil your gybe:
- When shifting the body to the inside of the turn the rig can be pulled across to leeward. In an extreme case steering with the rig will counteract the steering effect of the weight and the board will continue in a straight line. You should therefore push the rig to windward as you start to bear away.

If the second fault then follows the first, failure is inevitable.
- The sail is eased off too quickly and starts spilling wind. The effect of spilling wind from the sail increases the weather helm and pulls the board to windward. This causes it to lose speed as planing ceases, and the stern sinks thus increasing the braking action and the weather helm still more. The board luffs back onto its former course, flinging the windsurfer into the sea.
- The third common fault is leaning back in the turn. This loads the stern too hard, reducing the planing surface and causing the board to jump round out of control, or in less wind it will lose way and stop.

Make sure, therefore, that you lean forwards into the turn and push down on the boom. You can give yourself orders as a reminder, such as 'knee forward' or 'keep forward'. The reason for tending to lean back as described above is usually fear of the speed at which you are gybing. Confidence in your ability will conquer this.

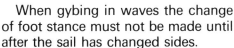

When gybing in waves the change of foot stance must not be made until after the sail has changed sides.

A variation of this manoeuvre is the **One-handed gybe** shown in stages:
- Check that there is room to leeward
- Slide your mast hand along the wishbone close up against the mast
- Place your back foot on the leeward edge of the board
- Bear away gradually while trying to pick up as much speed as possible
- Let go with sail hand

- Lean right into the turn, only holding the rig with the former mast hand
- Continue turning until you are on your new wind-abeam course
- Grab the mast with the old sail hand
- Start to sail on your new course
- Change the position of your feet.

When gybing it is essential to maintain sailing speed. This is therefore only suitable for average sailors when the wind is from astern, to provide the necessary speed.

The Beach Start

On page 19 we described how you should carry your board to the water without damaging it or getting in the way of anyone else.

The same applies to the beach start except that it is a little more difficult to master. The sailor enters the water together with his board and the rig. It is therefore necessary to carry the complete board with the rig already on it in a controlled way to the water's edge. This is the only way to start sailing in breakers, although flat sandy shores without large waves are also suitable for a beach start, not only because it is a neater way of entering the water but as a necessary stage in learning the water start. You will need to have mastered the beach start before you can sail out into waves breaking directly onto the shore, even if they are only a foot or so high.

There are three stages you must master for a successful beach start:
- You must take the fully rigged board into knee-deep water
- You must control the floating board
- You must succeed in climbing onto the board at the first attempt.

Carrying the board and rig to the water

In the ideal condition for a beach launch, which is a diagonally onshore wind, follow the sequence set out below and illustrated on page 47.
- Step the mast with the board lying at the water's edge, initially keeping the sail on the leeward side as a safety measure. Don't forget to attach the mast leash.

- Take hold of the mast just above the wishbone, keeping the rig in your hand with the mast to the front. Move round to the windward side of the board.
- Catch hold of the stern with your other hand and turn the board on its side.
Depending on the shape of your board, you can carry the stern in one of the following ways:
  - ○ Hold a broad stern by the skeg, turning the board on its side with the skeg towards you. You must keep out of the way of the fin, but the sail can swing out to leeward.
  - ○ Hold a narrow-ended board in front of the fin and turn it on its side.
  - ○ If you carry the board by a footstrap hold it by a side strap, otherwise as you push it into the water the bow will bury itself in the sand.
- Push the board into the water taking care that it stays vertical on edge and at right angles to the incoming waves.
- The board can be steered by pushing the bow to leeward or pulling it to windward with the mast hand, or easier still by taking a step to the right or left (as shown on page 47) while holding up the stern.
- When the water becomes knee-deep drop the stern and catch hold of the wishbone, pulling the sail in immediately. Shift your mast hand onto the boom as soon as you can.
- Watch the incoming waves carefully, bearing in mind the constantly changing depth of water and remembering that you must keep the fins and daggerboard off the bottom.

▲ Preparing for a beach start

▼ Pushing the board in by holding a footstrap

▲ Carrying a funboard: rig balances board

. . . or by supporting the stern.

Guiding the board

Standing in calm water on the windward side of the board and holding the rig with both hands on the boom, you have two ways to guide the board:

● You can bear away by tilting the rig to windward as if you were sailing (this is only possible to a limited extent as the sail can easily be pulled out of your hand); or alternatively by pushing the mast.

● Or you can luff by tilting the rig to leeward as if you were sailing, or by pulling the mast.

When launching from the beach your position on the board is particularly important; you should always stand near the stern. You will make starting easier if you can follow the movement of your board in shallow water, at the right moment counterbalancing any slight movement.

The main problem with a beach start is of course the waves. The board must be kept at right angles to the waves so that it can't be knocked round. You can only let small waves run under the board, but you must put slight pressure on the mast in order to keep the board in position.

In order to retain control in medium waves, from 1 to 3 ft high, you will need to keep your board at right angles to the waves, pulling the rig down firmly as you push it strongly forwards.

Unless the waves are very small, if your board is pushed off course by the waves and you lose control it is better to pull it back onto the shore and start the launch all over again.

Getting onto the board

Put your back foot onto the board and pull it towards you. Step up onto the board when the wind is abeam, or better still move from astern. Get your weight onto the board as soon as you can by leaning forward and pushing your knee forwards towards over the centre of the board. Haul in the sail at the same moment: you can then ease off slightly to get under way.

Even in a light breeze stepping up onto the board is not as easy as it looks. Attempting to pull yourself up by the sail often leads to failure: if the wind is light you must jump strongly onto the board and hold the rig as near vertical as possible with your arms out-stretched. You will need a good Force 4 wind before the sail will pull you up. Adjust the sail pressure by stretching your arms according to the strength of the wind.

1

4

Another cause of failure is incorrect positioning of the rig. While you are pushing your board out into the water the rig out to leeward will not affect you, but as soon as you put the board down it will luff up into the wind. In waves it can be difficult to regain control, so remember to push the rig quickly to windward.

When stepping onto the board put your foot on the fore-and-aft centreline so that the board doesn't tilt.

Faults and how to avoid them

The board is pushed sideways If your board is carried sideways hold the rig only by the mast, push or pull the bow into the next wave, stand close to the board and sufficiently far back that you can control it and push against the force of the waves with the mast hand on the foot of the mast. If necessary, take your board out of the water and prepare your beach start from the beginning again. This will avoid unnecessary damage to the equipment.

A fall in shallow water It is easy to get into a critical situation following a fall in waves, even in shallow water. Observe three important rules:

1. Never allow the board and rig to come between you and the waves. If you have been swept off the board, get out of danger by diving or going round to the shore side of the board. Many windsurfers have been badly hurt by having a board flung at them by the waves.

2. Lift the top of the mast immediately.
If the mast is lying pointing into the wind, lift the top and let the next wave pass under the board and rig to avoid any risk of breaking the mast.

When the clew is pointing into the wind you have a two choices. If the wind is strong and waves are coming in quick succession, lift the clew up to free the mast from the waves so they can pass under the board. If there is a sufficient interval between the waves you have time for another alternative: lift the clew and let it go again, allowing the sail to blow over, then catch hold of the mast as near the top as you can and walk into the waves.

3. Never let go of your board.
Always hang on. Riderless sailboards swept along by the waves can be a serious danger to bathers and sailors. If you let go of your board it will always be washed away from you by the waves: you can wade or swim after it, but you will not always be able to catch it. And if you are not there, who will hold up the top of the mast to keep it from breaking?

Landing

The most important point to bear in mind when sailing your board onto the beach is to avoid damaging it. In order not to be a danger to other windsurfers or bathers you must be able to beach your board in a controlled manner.

When sailing onto the beach you will need the lift of a wave to give you sufficient depth because waves draw the water away ahead of them.

Ease off the sail before you reach the spot where the water begins to be too shallow. Keeping your mast hand on the boom, step backwards to the windward side off the board. Grab the stern quickly before the next wave knocks the board round, or better still catch hold of a footstrap and lift the stern up. Push your board into the water's edge where you can turn it round and drag the board and rig up to a clear space. Now you can lay the sail to leeward, release the downhaul and outhaul lines, and you have come ashore in perfect order. The board and the rig have not been knocked about, the rig will not take off on its own and everything is ready for your next move.

Conserving your Strength

Many people assume that windsurfing requires a great deal of strength. We won't try to convince you that it doesn't need any strength at all, but if your technique is right the sport requires much less energy than is generally supposed. The correct technique requires the right sail position, relaxed body and arms, and maximum use of one's body weight to trim the board and sail. The fastest sailors expend the least energy.

Factors affecting speed are, once again: minimum water resistance and maximum sail power which must be high and forward. Water resistance is reduced by a balanced, well trimmed board, with the weight farther aft as the force of the wind increases. The key to optimum sail power is the correct position of the sail. The sail can only function at maximum effectiveness when it is at the correct angle to the apparent wind which should be between 15° and 20° to the sail's chord line. This is why we harden in the sail just enough to keep it from fluttering.

The foregoing also applies to funboards when planing in strong winds. A correctly positioned and tensioned sail produces maximum board speed because the area of the hull's wetted surface, which causes the drag, is reduced. When a board is planing to its maximum the correct sail position is fastest and least tiring to maintain.

Body position is also important in order to sail for long stretches at a time. The ideal stance is with the whole body straight; bends in the hips, knees or arms are an unnecessary drain on your strength. When wind conditions per- mit you should sail with outstretched arms placed at shoulder height and feet spread apart by the width of your hips and pointing into the sail; your weight should be evenly distributed. Having your feet so close together may make you feel a little unsteady to start with, but with practice you will find that it is not only less tiring but also gives more feel for the force of the wind.

Training yourself to develop a feel for the correct sail position in relation to the wind can be helped by keeping your hands quite close together until you can sail with only one hand. The sail can be sheeted in and let out quite precisely with only one hand simply by turning the upper body.

Ideal body position for sailing straight. Axis of shoulders parallel to chord line.

The Water Start

It is a delight to watch an expert starting from the water and an uninitiated spectator will have the impression that the water start requires no effort on the part of the sailor. This impression is not wrong, except that this apparently easy exercise requires a very good feel for wind and sail, practice and a great deal of experience on the water.

The best form of practice for the water start, and a prerequisite to performing it, is the beach start. The deeper the water in which you do your beach start the closer you are to making a water start.

As for the beach start, the water start consists of three stages which are shown on the pages 52–4.

Lifting the sail out of the water
Depending on the position of the board in relation to the wind, there are various ways of lifting the sail out of the

5

6

water easily. In every case you must tread water, at the same time trying to swim to windward, as you will have a problem trying to raise the sail unless the wind can get under and fill the sail from the luff.

If the sail is to leeward of the board with the clew pointing to the bow
Catch hold of the mast and pull it towards the stern until the wishbone lies across the board. Ideally the board and mast will be pointing in the same

direction and lying at right angles to the wind. Take hold of the mast with the mast hand just above the boom and pull it to windward, keeping it as low as possible. If the stern has sufficient buoyancy you can support yourself on it with your free hand.

If the sail is lying to windward of the board with the mast across the wind
Dive under the rig and catch hold of the mast above the boom. Push the mast up out of the water while swimming

3

4

7

8

strongly with your legs, letting the wind in under the luff. If the clew does not come up out of the water immediately, push the rig to windward.

If the sail is lying to windward with the mast pointing to windward and the clew pointing to the stern
Swim round to the top of the mast and by pulling on it bring the board round until the wind is blowing diagonally under the luff. Lift the luff out of the water while swimming strongly with your legs. When the sail is free of the water, while treading water move your hands along from the top of the mast to the boom.

Your sail will not always be in a favourable position in relation to the board, but here is a tip if:
● the rig is to windward with the clew pointing to the bow, *or*
● the rig is to leeward with the clew pointing towards the. stern.
Swim round to pull the clew slightly into the wind, lift it and allow it to flop over. Now your sail is either to windward or leeward in position to get out of the water using one or other of the methods described above.

Guiding the board
While it may not be obvious to a spectator, the legs play a major part in controlling and directing boards. When the sail is out of the water put both hands on the wishbone, allowing the sail to become more upright thus carrying its own weight and taking the strain off your legs. As with the beach start the safest position is beside the stern and to windward. Get your back foot up as soon as you can, letting the other leg hang down vertically.

Some techniques for steering the board from the water.
Bearing away
● Steer the rig as if you were sailing by tilting the mast to windward (only possible to a limited extent)
● Pull your back foot in towards your body
● Exert sideways pressure on the foot of the mast
● With a combination of your foot coming in towards the body and sideways pressure on the mast foot.
Luffing up
● Steer the rig as if you were sailing by tilting the mast to leeward
● Pushing your back foot away from your body and
● Easing off the sail until the luff flaps.

Getting up onto the board
In order to get onto your board turn it until the wind is from the side or nearer the stern. With your back foot on the stern pull it in close to your body. The trick is to increase the power of the sail, not only until the wind takes it allowing you to guide the board but so that it also lifts you out of the water. For this the sail must be as near vertical as possible. Your mast hand should be holding the boom no more than a hand's width from the sail's centre of pressure. To get going lean the upper part of your body forwards while your sail hand pulls the sail in. Only when your body is right over the board should you straighten the leg on which you are standing. Ease off slightly before you sail away.

If there is not much wind and your board is a sinker, kicking hard in the water with your other leg will help you to get onto the board.

Water starting in strong or light winds

It is easier to get the sail out of the water in a strong wind than in a light breeze. The problems occur as you get up onto the board and start to sail away. The stronger the wind the broader your reach will have to be before you get up. Put your back foot as far back towards the stern as you can and ease off the boom as soon as the sail lifts you up. In strong winds you will be able to adjust the power of the sail very readily.

The converse applies in a light wind: the power of the sail must be increased by having the rig more vertical and shortening the leverage. Hold the mast with the mast hand and if there is very little wind hold the foot of the sail with your sail hand. You will not be able to climb aboard until you can get your back leg, or perhaps both legs, across the board. If there is still not enough wind you can let the rig hang out to leeward and pull up by the mast.

For a successful water start:

● When lifting the sail never push the mast up: instead, you should tread water and pull the sail round to windward keeping it low.

● When guiding your board don't only steer with the rig but use the pull of the sail assisted by your foot on the stern and your leg in the water.

● When getting up onto the board never pull yourself up on the sail but put it as near vertical as possible and in the correct sailing position, pull the stern in towards you, and with your front leg increasing the resistance in the water and outstretched front arm let the sail pull you up out of the water.

It is easier to learn the water start on some boards than others. A short wishbone (up to 2.30 m), fathead or powerhead sails, a fully extended daggerboard and a boom set fairly low (not above eye level) facilitate accomplishing this wet exercise.

Water start in little wind: holding the foot of the sail and the mast

Water start with clew forward following an unsuccessful gybe

Sailing with a Trapeze

It is no coincidence that the section on using a trapeze comes just before we deal with safety. This important aid to conserving your strength and prolonging your endurance on the water can also greatly contribute to your safety.

We must, however, qualify this by saying, 'Only sail with a trapeze in winds of a force that you are capable of handling without it.' A trapeze will not help you to sail better: it can only extend the time you can sail.

We do most earnestly recommend that all windsurfers who have passed the elementary stages get used to the trapeze, even if it means overcoming a fear of getting entangled.

Equipment

Trapeze harness has attracted some rather fanciful inventors. We recommend the simple Hawaiian belt as the most useful. A practical *trapeze belt* should:

● Reach your lumbar vertebra at the back and be firm enough to support your lower back
● Be padded and have broad, firm belting around it at the main load-bearing points
● To increase its value as a safety aid, be coloured fluorescent red or orange and incorporate a small rucksack for extra clothing or safety gear; the rucksack should have a strong zip and drain holes for water
● Have its hook fixed to a wide front chest strap or a 'spreader bar' which will avoid constricting your ribcage by the pull on the belt
● Have a quick-release buckle in case the hook becomes inextricably tangled in the trapeze line.

Having found a harness that conforms to these requirements, always try it on, hook it up and lean back for a few minutes to test it. A well cut six-point harness will distribute the weight over your back better than a four-point belt.

The *trapeze line* should be at least 8 mm in diameter, of strong pre-stretched stiff rope. You will need a piece about 1.30–1.50 m long ($4\frac{1}{2}$–5 ft) on each side of the boom.

Attaching the line

Ideally, your sailing technique should not be affected by the use of a trapeze. From this it follows that the ends of the line should not be fastened to the boom farther apart than the width of your shoulders. Find the position on the boom at which you can hold the rig with one hand in a moderate wind. The correct points to attach the line are 20–30 cm to either side of this. You can then hold the wishbone just outside the line when using your hands, but the use of the trapeze will not distort the feel of the rig.

Whether your harness lines are attached to the wishbone with jam cleats, straps or sleeves, you should check whether they allow the lines to slip sideways. If they are not secure, attach the lines with trapeze knots or rolling hitches (p 68, 69) which are easily tied and quick to untie. Leave the lines long enough for you to sail comfortably with nearly straight arms, holding the boom at shoulder level.

Hooking and unhooking

Most trapeze harnesses allow you to sail with the hook pointing up or down.

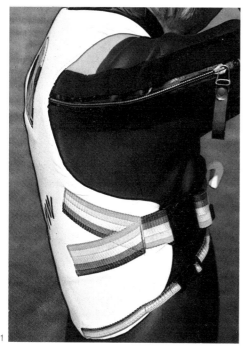

Figs. 1 and 2: *Good six-point harness*

Fig. 3: *With a well-fitting harness you can sail one-handed even in strong winds*

Fig. 4: *Trying to hook on with a line that is too short*

Fig. 5: *Arms are shoulder width apart*

There are advantages and disadvantages to both methods, and windsurfers are divided in their support. When you first start using a trapeze experiment with both ways.

To hook onto the line pull the wishbone up and towards you in a circular, quick movement. The line will then swing from below up into the book. You can practise this method of hooking up while on shore.

To unhook yourself, also pull the boom in towards you to allow the line to drop down and out of the hook once the tension is taken off.

You can try hooking on and off easily and quickly while on land, but the difficulty of windsurfing with a trapeze lies in the fear that in an emergency one will not have time to get free of the harness. So we have set out some practice exercises which should remove any fear of being dragged down by the harness.

When falling you should in any case keep both hands on the boom. The greatest danger of injury comes from a catapult fall.

If you fall to windward and are still in the harness, push the line out of the hook with your hand. Don't panic: you have enough time to do this, even if you are underneath the sail. If you fall to leeward and are still holding onto the boom, you will be lying on your front across the rig so you will be able to pull the line out of the hook.

If you have let go of the boom you will probably have executed a somersault with a half twist and finish lying on the sail with your feet towards the top of mast. You must undo the quick-release buckle to take the tension off the line and push it out of the hook.

Exercises

● Practice hooking yourself in and out, first of all on land, then with slackened sail and finally with a fully sheeted in sail.

● Move to and fro along the line until the pull on both arms is even; let go first with one hand then the other before practising with both hands free: the rig will keep in position without your hands.

● Practice the starting and stopping exercise without the trapeze, making sure that you can ease off and harden in the sail just by turning your body.

● Sail inside the wishbone, pulling it down until it is no higher than the line of your shoulder. When you are inside the boom you are forced to control the sail by turning the upper part of your body.

● Sail while holding the rig only by the trapeze lines.

● While sailing closehauled hang back into your harness and let yourself be pulled into a fall into the sail to leeward: so long as you keep your hands on the boom you will not come to harm. Practice this several times and it will give you confidence for such falls.

● Dive under the sail as it is lying in the water; when you have done this a few times you will be able to do it quite slowly with your eyes open.

● In a moderate wind hook on and let go of the boom, first with one hand then the other; you will soon see that you can haul the sail in and let it out without using your hands, simply by the movement of your body.

Safety

The more expert a windsurfer you become the more you will pit yourself against difficult conditions; your equipment and your body will be tested to a greater extent.

You have no control over external conditions such as weather, tides and their related currents, therefore it is all the more essential for you to be fully informed about them.

If you only sail on a small local lake you may feel that this warning is over-cautious, but even then you will take certain precautions. You know which are the swimming areas, you are aware from which direction storms are likely to come, and you will also be aware of the nature of the bottom near the shore where you can launch and land your board. You have always been able to correct a bad decision by going back and putting on a smaller sail or warmer clothing if necessary. On large areas of water or at sea, if you have chosen too large a sail and the conditions prevent your being able to return to the shore you are at the mercy of the elements; even if it is not very rough, if it is cold and you are inadequately dressed you may become too chilled to function well enough to get back to shore.

The ten safety rules here and the hints on how to manage if you have failed to observe them should help you to sail safely in unfamiliar waters also.

1. Knowledge of local conditions
Local people, sailing schools or clubs can save you finding out the hard way. Pay particular attention to:
- local weather and wind conditions, any usual changes during the day
- local storm warning signals, or prohibitions against giving out
- the times of low and high tide, and when tidal streams change direction
- potentially dangerous currents caused by the contours of the shore or bottom, e.g. rip-tides, overfalls.

Windsurfers may be required to observe certain regulations protecting both themselves and the environment.

Ten Safety Rules
1. Learn about local conditions and regulations.
2. Take adequate clothing to protect you against cold, from the water or from wind.
3. Check your equipment every time you go sailing.
4. Use a safety line (leash) to tie the rig to the board, and take a long towline with you.
5. Allow yourself time to study the wind and weather. Do not set out to sea in strong offshore winds.
6. Never go out on large areas of water alone without telling somebody.
7. Do not overestimate your own strength. Select the size of sail carefully and allow for rest periods. Don't continue until you are exhausted.
8. Avoid congested and busy waters with commercial traffic or swimmers.
9. Improve your sailing ability and learn the emergency and rescue drills.
10. Always stay with your board.

2. Protection against the cold

Your body cools off five times faster in water than in the air. Even when standing up on your board, evaporation from wind and spray can lower your body temperature to such an extent that all your internal reserves of strength are used up just in keeping warm. Co-ordination, mental concentration and judgement all deteriorate as one gets cold, often without it being realized. If you wear a jacket without a strap between the legs to prevent its being pulled up, wear your wetsuit or trapeze harness over it.

A 6m long towrope stowed round the boom. Other short spare lines would fit on the other side.

3. Check your equipment

Use the checklist on page 16 every time you sail to make sure that your board and rig are in good order. The more conscientiously you do this the less likely will be an emergency due to faulty equipment. If you make a practice of carrying out a routine check at the end of every day's sailing, you will spot defects and have time to remedy them before your next outing.

4. Joining the board and rig and towrope

Offshore your board will be your liferaft so you should be able to reach it after a fall, and it must therefore be impossible for it to be washed away. As long as it is attached to the board, the mast and sail will act as a sea anchor and keep it from blowing away from you. The board will be under less strain in rough water if the mast leash is fixed near the bow.

You can carry a 6 m long towline in your trapeze bag or wound round the boom. If you need to be towed it will give you more space between your board and your rescuer, and reduce the danger of injury from a fall. If one of the sail lines should break you can replace it with the towline, or carry some shorter lines for this purpose.

5. Study the wind and weather

Assess the local conditions using information from local sailors, weather reports and forecasts. Wind and waves in particular will be affected by local topography; features such as buildings, cliffs or high banks will deflect, block and act as a brake on the wind.

In an onshore wind there will be a windward lull near the shore. This disturbance in the normal airflow reaches to windward up to eight times the height of the obstruction. In an offshore wind the wind shadow downwind of the shore can reach twenty times as far, so from the shore it is impossible to judge the wind speed out on open water. To try to assess it look for an open beach without high trees, houses, dunes or a steeply shelving shore. Or ask sailors who have come in. Anyone who sets out to sea on a board in an offshore wind is asking for trouble. Beginners who intend only to sail parallel to the shore may also find themselves blown out to sea and unable to get back.

6. Do not sail alone
Many windsurfers and other sailors owe their lives to observing this rule on open water. If you have informed the sailing school or a friend of your plans, if you get into difficulties you can hope for rescue. But to avoid an unnecessary search do remember to let them know when you come in.

7. Do not overestimate your capabilities
It is particularly difficult to judge your capability when you sail again after a break. It is better to use a smaller sail to start with and begin with a few turns round the harbour, then come ashore for a rest. You can then change your sail, check the lines and warm up.

If you realize that the manoeuvres you are carrying out do not go as well as you expected, this indicates that your strength is not what you thought it was and you should take a rest. Or, your technique may seem all right but your endurance may be reduced.

8. Avoid commercial vessels
Near shipping channels a breakdown is always dangerous. If you become becalmed or get into a lull or other unforseen circumstance you may drift into the path of a ship unable to see you or take avoiding action in time. This is why windsurfing is prohibited in shipping channels and some commercial waters and in the interests of safety you should keep a safe distance from these areas.

9. Become a better sailor and know your emergency drill
See pages 62–5, on emergencies.

10. Always stay with your board
Sailboards are unsinkable. You will not drown if you stay on your board, and you will not cool down as quickly as if you were in the water. Sitting on your board, you can signal for help or paddle to the shore. Sinkers (boards with a volume below about 100 litres) do not have sufficient buoyancy to support you if they are not moving, however. This fact should be clearly marked by the board manufacturer. Even on a floater you can get very cold indeed, and may be there a long time: again, extra warm and windproof clothing becomes vital.

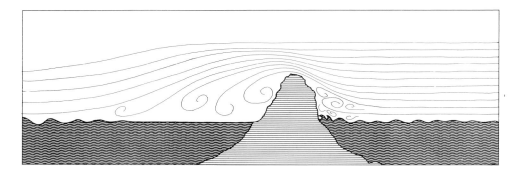

What to Do In an Emergency

The best advice we can give to *prevent* emergencies is to observe the ten safety rules, above. You may nevertheless find yourself in difficulties and be required to help yourself or others.

● If you are becalmed, roll up the sail and stow your rig flat as if for a tow and paddle to shore.
● If you are exhausted, you will have to take a tow or be picked up by rescuers if you are unlikely to be driven ashore by a favourable tide and/or wind.
● If your equipment breaks you can often carry out emergency repairs as described below, but if the repair is not likely to be effective and you might be driven farther offshore it is better to call for help in time.

Emergency repairs
A sail can tear at the top, the tack and the clew. A tear along a seam will not entirely impede your ability to get back as the rest of the sail will continue to hold the wind. If the sail is torn at the tack you will also get home without difficulty. If the top of the sleeve has given way slacken the downhaul, tie shut the luff sleeve below the reinforced head of the sail and retighten the downhaul moderately.

If the sail tears at the clew, bundle it up as though you wanted to wring it out and tie it round with the loose end of the outhaul using a sheet bend. On a modern sail with a high-cut clew, tie the lashing as tight as you can around inside the reinforced corner and tighten up the outhaul again.

Your boom breaks
The modern aluminium wishbone will probably only bend if it is damaged, so you will be able to sail home on the other side. If an end fitting breaks lash your spare line round both broken ends of the wishbone.

Broken mast
If the mast splits just above the foot wet your spare line and stretch it before tying ten half-hitches tightly round the mast. If the mast breaks higher up by the wishbone you will have to paddle home.

The mast foot or joint breaks
Use your spare line to lash the broken ends together as tightly as possible. Or you could lash the mast to the top of the dagger. Spare line tied tightly round the board can serve as a form of emergency mast attachment.

Broken daggerboard
If you still have the broken piece push it through the slot and wedge it tight with your spare line, so that it cannot work lose. But it is usually possible to get home without a centreboard.

A fin or a fin box breaks
If you find yourself having to sail with only one fin or without a daggerboard, sail before the wind as much as you can, or paddle.

But so long as your board has a daggerboard, or if you have one fin left, you should be able to sail home.

Stowing your board for rescue
You may find it difficult to dissemble your board and rig for a rescue operation in rough water and a strong

wind if you have not already practised on land, and then in calmer water. We recommend the following as the safest method:

- Sit astride the board.
- Pull the mast foot out of its socket and pull the clew towards you.
- Untie the clew outhaul on one side and fold the wishbone up to the top of the mast.
- Roll the sail up tightly from the foot, keeping your hands close to the clew. If necessary take out the battens and roll them up in the sail.
- Tie the boom to the mast with the loose end of the outhaul and wind the rest of the outhaul round the mast and sail working down towards the foot of the mast.
- Undo the uphaul from the foot of the mast and wind it round the mast and sail working towards the top of the mast. Finally tie it with the shock cord so it doesn't come unwound.

Paddling

You should only lay the rolled-up rig along the board if you have a spare line or strap to lash it down with, otherwise the rig is likely to slip off into the water. You will be better advised to leave the mast stepped even if the trailing rig acts as a brake.

If you swim the board forward by kicking with your legs instead of using your arms you risk getting too cold.

In a wind no stronger than Force 4 it will be difficult to make headway against the wind. If you are likely to be in danger you should ask for a tow or signal for help.

The International Distress Signal

Sit or kneel on your board and wave both outstretched arms up and down at your sides.

You will be more easily seen if you stand on the board holding on to the uphaul and swing a brightly coloured (preferably not multi-coloured) object, such as a harness or jacket, round in a circle. When sailing at sea we recommend carrying distress flares or smoke signals. If in danger set off red flares, but only if you think they are likely to be seen. If you do set off a flare, leave your sail rigged and lying in the water, where it is more likely to be seen from above. Also, it will slow your drift if the wind is in the wrong direction.

You should not be in any doubt as to the significance of these international distress signals. They mean that the sailor is in **serious and imminent danger and requires immediate assistance**. It is obligatory for anyone who sees them to take action within the limits of their own safety. If you should see a distress signal and are not able to carry out a rescue yourself, you must report the circumstance at the nearest harbour or to the police or Coastguard with precise details of time and position.

Towing

If paddling will not get you home a tow can be a useful form of rescue. You should practise towing another board

and being towed so that you will be able to manage in an emergency. You will be moving twice the weight. When tacking the leeway will be much greater and your manoeuvres will be severely hindered by the towed board. The best method is to attach a towrope from the bow of the towed board to the foot of the mast of the towing board. If neither of you have a towrope you can make a tow bar from the rolled-up rig (see photo). Fit the mast foot into the second socket or tie it to the downhaul.

It is very difficult for the towing board to make way if the sailor under tow is holding on by a footstrap or daggerboard strap. Irrespective of whether the board is being towed on the leeward or windward side every changeover of the sail will push the boards apart and the towed windsurfer will have to change sides.

If you are only being towed for a short distance and you are in a hurry, you can just release the outhaul of your sail and let the rig drag in the water.

Rescue

If a sailor is rescued by a ship's lifeboat or a rescue service boat he may be lifted

on deck with davits or a hoist. Do exactly as you are told by the person in charge of the rescue. Do not stay on your board or you will be in danger of being injured by the propellers.

If rescued by a helicopter a belt, basket or stretcher will be lowered, either with or without an assistant. Before catching hold of the rescue wire, let the end touch the water to discharge the electricity generated by unwinding. Never try to hold onto your board or tie the wire to it or you will endanger the lives of the rescue crew.

Strap the rescue belt round your body under your arms. Bring the closing cuff which prevents the body from slipping out round in front of your chest. Keep your arms down and close to your body when you are lifted into the air to prevent slipping out of the loop.

In some countries anyone who has caused an emergency by *gross negligence* is liable for the cost of rescue.

There is no alternative to abandoning the rig and swimming ashore with the board.

Ropework and Knots

Ropes are made of natural fibres such as hemp and sisal and artificial fibres such as nylon, Terylene, Dacron or polyethylene. Natural fibre ropes are now seldom used in sailing and never for windsurfing, although they have the great advantage that knots tied in them will not slip. But they rot very quickly if not cared for and the ends must be whipped. After cutting synthetic fibre rope all you usually need do is melt the end to prevent it from unravelling, though some need whipping also.

In addition to knowing about the different materials from which ropes are made it is also important to recognize the various ways they are constructed. A line of a particular thickness might be laid (twisted) or plaited, and many types of rope are available either pre-stretched or unstretched. Laid ropes are seldom used in windsurfing although they do not stretch much and hold well in jam cleats. Lines are usually 6 mm thick, pre-stretched and plaited and without a core. Trapeze lines should ideally contain some Kevlar as they need to be stiff with minimal stretch and will not chafe. They should be at least 8 mm.

Knots and how to tie them

The sequences on the next pages show you how to tie several of the most useful knots.

Knots and hitches should have the following properties:
- be easy and quick to tie
- hold well under load without slipping or jamming
- be quick and easy to undo.

All knots are a combination of two basic elements, the *bight* and the *loop*, as shown.

When making a knot you should only use one end of a piece of line. To practise, mark the free ends with tape or tie off the other ones.

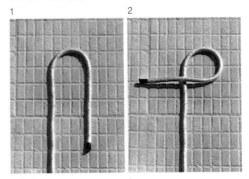

Bight   Loop

The mast hitch is used to tie the boom inhaul line to the mast. The photos on page 11 also show the **overhand** or **stopper knot** in the end of the inhaul.

The figure-of-eight knot in the end of a rope is another type of stopper knot and prevents it from slipping out.

Reef or square knots are used to tie together two ropes of equal thickness. (If they are under strain, use a **sheet bend** instead.)

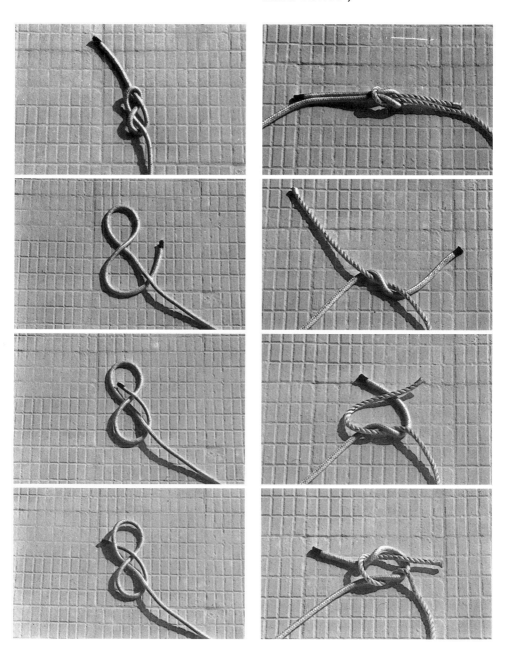

The bowline is a loop that will not slip and pull tight. Used on the downhaul and outhaul, and very useful generally.

The rolling hitch doesn't slip when pulled sideways. Used to secure the inhaul and may join mast and boom.

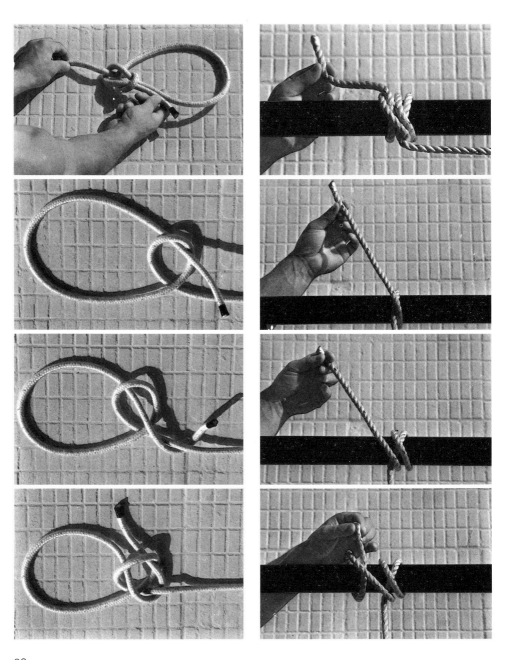

Trapeze knots used to tie the ends of trapeze lines can be loosened by pushing with the thumb and slipping along the boom.

Round turns with two half-hitches are easy to tie and have various uses.

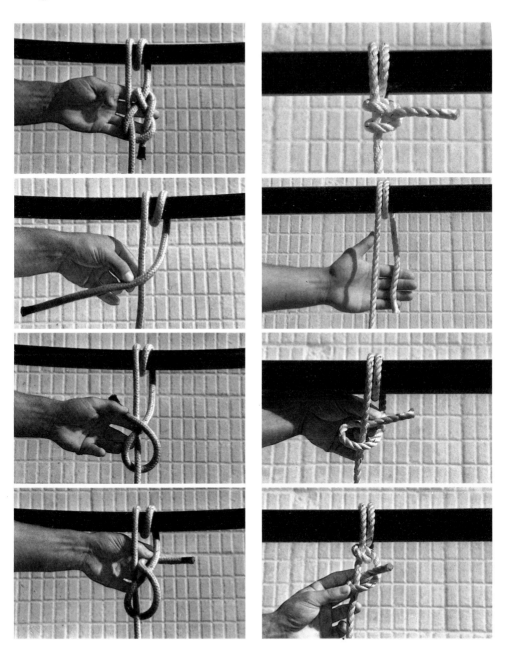

Clove hitch, used to tie off ends of outhaul lines next to cleats. Generally useful, best with steady tension.

Sheet bend, to join two ropes especially if under strain (towropes etc) or of unequal size. Secure but can be easily undone.

Windsurfing Theory and Background

However much one concentrates on the practical aspects of windsurfing, there is no escaping the fact that attention must be paid to learning about many aspects over and above carrying out the various movements.

This broader knowledge includes many subjects, from knowing about equipment and materials to enable one to evaluate the relative merits of the great range of boards, rigs and accessories on the market; or the dynamics of sailing; or the rules and regulations which govern all pleasure craft and which you must know for your own safety. A good, advanced windsurfer is not therefore necessarily the greatest expert at sailing his board, but the one who in addition to his 'performing' expertise has adequate knowledge and seamanship for the exercise of his sport and to conduct himself safely among other craft.

Knowing the Equipment

In this section we look at the boards themselves and also examine sails and rigs, clothing and other essentials, and also some less vital accessories.

Types of boards

In the short history of windsurfing boards have now divided themselves into four categories: displacement, all-round, all-round fun and funboards. All designs either belong to or are combinations of these basic categories.

Displacement boards, sometimes called roundboards, can be recognized by their length and rounded underwater shape, which facilitates speed and the ability to sail closer to the wind than other types. Due to their instability they are not easy for beginners and the long daggerboard increases a tendency to capsize. Those conforming to IYRU Div. II rules have a class to themselves for racing. On conventional triangular courses displacement boards are far superior. Pan Am Cup boards developed for open sea racing and breaking waves are also displacement types. The underside of the bow is rounded and rockered (curved up) and the wetted surface flattens off towards the stern. The daggerboard can be fully extended or angled up.

All-round boards are relatively stable, flatter, not over-sensitive designs that are highly suitable for beginners, enabling them to learn and progress in all aspects of the sport. They can be sailed fast in gentle and moderate breezes, compete in races, and depending on the make are suitable for freestyle. All-rounders can be sailed with a degree of success in waves, but they are unsuitable for strong winds.

All-round funboards are designed to allow windsurfers who have acquired average skill to progress to the level of funboard and heavy weather sailing. They are around 3.3–3.5 m long with daggerboards that can be fully extended and large fins, providing good performance characteristics in high winds. They can be footsteered by weighting the outside rail when the daggerboard is extended, or the inside edge when it is retracted. The all-round concept embraces so many variations in behaviour and displacement that it is important to choose carefully to get a board which suits one's weight and capabilities.

Funboards have only fins, not daggerboards, and are about 2.5–3 m long. Their short shape and light weight give them remarkable speed and manoeuvrability in skilled hands, but they demand mastery of short-board technique. So-called **marginals** are a little less demanding than **radicals** in this respect. Funboards are the only safe boards for windsurfing in breaking waves. Size is a very important factor. Around 100 litres volume they can just about support the weight of an 'average' man of 75 kg (165 lbs or 12 stone) and the rig: the board will only just float under this weight, giving rise to the name **semi-floater** or **semi-sinker**. Boards less than 100 L in volume must be regarded as sinkers for most people as they no longer support their weight unless they are under way.

A selection of boards used by Robby Naish and Peter Cabrinha in the San Francisco 1983 Wave-riding final. From right to left: boards 1 and 3 are squashtail wingers; boards 2 and 4 are fishtail wingers.

How are sailboards made?

There is an inner plastic foam core, for stiffening and buoyancy, of polyurethane or polystyrene and a tough outer skin of either hard-setting plastic such as fibre-reinforced polyester or epoxy resin, or of thermoplastic, which is hot-moulded, such as ABS, ASA and polyethelene. Composites can be reinforced with glass or carbon fibre, Kevlar or various mixtures of these.

Thermoplastics are industrial plastics which can only be moulded by sophisticated machinery. They can be made rapidly and cheaply in long production runs, but for the purchaser have the drawback that some repairs are more difficult. Thermoplastic boards are less likely to be damaged, however (this applies to a lesser extent to ABS and ASA), while polyethylene boards are virtually indestructible. Thermoplastics are so tough that there is no need for fibre reinforcement, but to obtain comparable rigidity they require a thicker outer skin than the harder duroplastics.

Finishing Manufactured boards have their hulls made in female moulds. This produces two halves of a board which are then stuck together along the edges and filled with polyurethane foam. Good boards have reinforcement along the seams.

Individually made boards are custom-finished, which is almost exactly the reverse procedure to the moulding method. The board gets its desired length and shape from cutting and rubbing down a ready-made blank foam core. This is then covered with glassfibre or other reinforcement and coated with resin. Once cured, the board is smoothed down and mast sockets, fins, footstraps etc are fitted. Small builders use this method for their customers' special requirements and large companies also use this system to make prototypes for new models. By using this method a windsurfer can build a do-it-yourself board to his own requirements at relatively low cost, though he will need quite a lot of time for the job. (**Sailboards Custom Made** by Hans Fichtner and Michael Garff, published by Stanford Maritime, describes the complete DIY building procedure.) Few first attempts result in the perfect board, however.

A board may have a variety of shapes which will affect its performance. The ability of a board to sail in a curve will be greatly influenced by the roundness or sharpness of the underwater edges. You should also be aware of the influence on sailing characteristics of the board by the degree of scoop, as the 'rocker' is called at the bow; the rocker being the amount of curvature between the bow and the stern. Hull volume, width and numerous other variables all affect handling.

The daggerboard and fins

The influence of the daggerboard and fins on a board's performance is far greater than would appear from their size, and their importance was not appreciated in the early years of windsurfing. Increasing attention is now being paid to these two aspects of board design. The daggerboard reduces leeway by counteracting the sideways movement on courses across or at an angle to the wind. In many cases the fins also fulfil this function, in addition to helping to provide directional stability in conjunction with a daggerboard. Stability and sail balance are also affected by the position, angle, depth and area of the daggerboard.

The effectiveness of daggerboards and fins is only partially determined by their surface area. In a similar manner to the wing of an airplane, the forces acting on the appendages of a sailboard result from the dynamics of water flow. The profile and cross-section shapes of daggerboards and fins are therefore much more important than their size: a good shape will clearly produce more lift and less drag than a badly designed one. Important points in fin design are the ratio between the length and width of the profile, the position of the thickest part of the section and the taper and angle of the edges. Racing fins are sometimes fitted with fences designed to reduce the vertical flow of air down the fin (ventilation).

In the box below you can see some variously shaped fins. The sweptback and kanga cock variations are, however, relics of the early days of funboards as they have been found to have a marked braking effect.

Centreboards such as the plain straight-through dagger or the fixed angled storm version are also rarely seen on new boards today. Most current designs incorporate a fully variable system which can be fully or partly retracted into the hull.

The sail
Sailcloth of Terylene or Dacron and the more exotic laminated or 'pure' Mylar are both used. Terylene is much cheaper than Mylar and its long-term performance is well known, but it also wears out faster. Only woven sailcloth sails may be permitted in some competitions.

Mylar sails can produce speeds around 20 per cent faster. Due to the fact that Mylar does not stretch and even under strain will not deform, the curvature and the position of the fullness of the sail and the pattern of pressure of the wind over the sail's

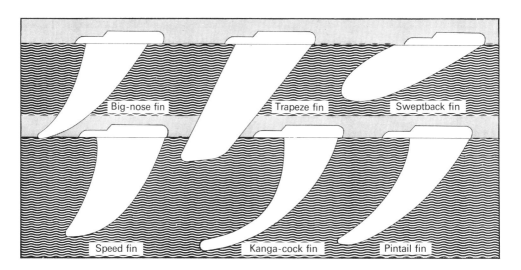

Big-nose fin   Trapeze fin   Sweptback fin

Speed fin   Kanga-cock fin   Pintail fin

surface can be precisely determined. It is therefore possible to sail a more accurate course with a Mylar sail because the pressure over the sail remains stable.

Sail selection

A windsurfer selects his sail according to the board he is using, the strength of the wind and the wave conditions. All types of displacement and all-round boards can use sails with a low clew. As the daggerboard and fins of all-round funboards and small funboards are placed farther towards the stern, the rigs for these boards need a higher clew to prevent the end of the wishbone from catching the waves when sailing fast downwind or water starting. Both types of sail are available in a variety of areas and cuts.

Mast and boom lengths will also vary, so always make sure that the sail fits in your boom exactly and that the foot is not more than 10 cm (4 in) above the foot of the mast when the downhaul is fully tightened. You will thereby avoid great variations in the position of the centre of effort, and loss of speed due to pressure equalization under the foot of the sail.

Even the best sail will only produce optimum results when correctly set and matched to the right mast. Most windsurfers underestimate the reduction in performance caused by neglecting these points: a loss of up to 20 per cent of a board's potential sailing speed can easily result.

Mast and boom

Both the mast and the boom must be sealed to prevent water entering, as if they fill with water they will become very heavy and difficult to pull out of the water.

The decisive factor in chosing a mast is the sail you intend to use. The curvature of the luff must match the stiffness of the mast otherwise the sail will develop creases which even the most skilled trimming cannot remove.

If your mast is made of any material other than aluminium, e.g. GRP (glass-fibre reinforced plastic), you should check it regularly for cracks where the inhaul is fastened round it and at the foot. The points where the boom is most inclined to break are where it joins the end fittings and at the trapeze lines. Check these areas after a catapult fall with a trapeze.

When choosing a boom for your board you should take account of the stiffness of the boom, in addition to the length and curvature of the two side tubes. A very curved, flexible boom will make controlling your rig more difficult. If you buy a variable-length boom keep a careful watch on the extension. Telescoping ends secured with a screwed connecting piece tend to give way under the strain of a strong pull. The telescoping end should not contribute additional weight, as every ounce out at the end of the boom is increased by the lever effect, making the rig more unwieldy to handle.

Mast foot and the universal joint

The rubber universal joint has found widespread acceptance on sailboards as the flexible coupling between the mast foot fitting and the mast. The universal joint must always be freely moveable around the part of the mast foot which fits into the board. The harder types of rubber are liable either to unscrew or twist and shear off.

Mast feet constructed under the German DIN standard must have a safety release (similar in principle to a ski binding) or a quick-release system; this can be done for sliding mast tracks. Some other foot fittings are adjustable for ease of release and can be set so that the mast and board are very unlikely to come apart accidentally.

The rig safety line or leash is a 'must' for windsurfers. This line keeps the rig attached to the board after the mast has come unstepped. A board free of its rig can blow away faster than you can possibly swim after it. Do not rely on a piece of wire to hold the leash to the mast foot, as with the first really hard pull it is likely to snap. The retaining line should be attached to the mast by one and a half round turns and a

A mast extension will be required for sails with extra long luff. Unless you are sailing directly into the waves your

Telescopic boom extension

mast extension should be no longer than necessary for a well trimmed luff otherwise you will produce awkward leverage on the rig. You will also lose power from the sail as the air flows away under the foot.

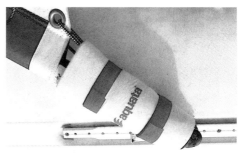

bowline; the other end should always be fastened to the bow so that even if the board hits the waves vertically or is caught in breakers it will offer less resistance and thus the line will not be under so much strain.

Mast protection If you have a custom-made board you should buy a padded sleeve that fits round the mast below the sail. Unless you have fitted this the mast can damage the board when the rig is lying in the water. By protecting the mast you cushion the pressure on the board.

Trapeze attachments For those who dislike tying knots there are various fittings. Make sure they will not slip when the trapeze line is slack and not taking your weight. Avoid hard clamps. The best type are those with Velcro strips but if they get dirty they lose their grip.

Footstraps For precise control of the board with your feet, footstraps are essential. The most important features are their stiffness, also when wet, and adaptability in height. Enough stiffness for the loop to stand up off the board is vital for comfort and safety, as nothing is so annoying as having got away to a good strong-wind start and then having to fish around with your feet to find your way into the straps. The loop should be sufficiently big to allow the toes to just come through to the other

side. Your instep can be badly rubbed if the strap is too large, and in a fall having the foot so far in can cause serious injuries. You should not be tempted to have more footstraps on your board than are really necessary or your movements will be hampered. Three or four pairs are enough.

Clothing

A wetsuit is essential for windsurfing in our latitudes and together with the board and rig must be regarded as part of the basic kit. When buying your windsurfing clothing do not let your purchase be governed only by the cost, or the money you save initially could be more than offset by subsequent expense. Even though the material of two different wetsuits may appear almost identical, the differences can be so great that one will only last you a season while another will stand up to years of wear. You should bear the following points in mind:

● waterproofing of the neoprene
● stitching method
● effective protection against cold
● no irritation when next to the skin
● resistance to tearing, deterioration from sunlight, weathering and sea water
● good stretching qualities allowing all the necessary body movements without hindering or tearing.

Double-lined wetsuits are proof against snagging but they do not always have sufficient stretch; they dry more slowly and consequently are not as warm as single-lined suits. If you intend to continue windsurfing into late autumn and winter or in early spring you should acquire a drysuit or a blind-stitched 'dry wetsuit'.

Footwear

Many windsurfers wear a body belt or kidney belt to keep their lumbar region warm, but actually the kidneys will not be chilled so much by cold on the back as from cold limbs, especially the feet. Shoes not only protect from injury to the feet but also provide warmth. The best shoes to wear for windsurfing should be as thin as possible with good traction on the soles while providing maximum warmth. Really solid board-riding boots tend to be clumsy.

Looking After your Equipment

As the owner of a windsurfing board you are fortunate enough to have in your possession a piece of equipment which needs practically no maintenance. By its very simplicity it will last for a long time. There are only a few basic rules and obvious precautions which you should bear in mind.

The sailboard, dagger and fins

The most important rule to ensure a long life for these items is to avoid contact with the land or bottom. When coming ashore on your board, step off in good time and you will prevent the daggerboard or fins from breaking or being ripped out of the board; you will also avoid scraping their edges or the bottom of the board on sharp stones. If you should hole your board you will have to keep the water out or the foam will be damaged and possibly come away from the skin. You should return to the shore immediately with even the smallest hole in a board and seal it with sticky tape. Later you can make it fully watertight with a resin filler or GRP.

Cracks in the gelcoat should also be taped over and made good as soon as possible. Water will seep into the laminate via even hair cracks and when the next frosty weather comes it will begin to break away.

Never lay the board on its fins on the shore, and always put it in the shade if you can. Some boards are sensitive to exposure to ultra-violet light and weather and become brittle or faded.

The mast and boom

The mast and boom are also relatively maintenance-free. If the covering on the boom should work loose it should be stuck back again immediately, otherwise it will soon tear. In order to stick it down inject an adhesive under the grip material and twist it backwards and forwards to spread the adhesive. Push the grip into the correct position and allow the adhesive to set, perhaps taping the material in place in the meantime.

To protect the mast and mast foot from splitting you can fit wide hose clips round the end of the mast, but wrap some plastic insulating tape round the bottom end of the mast first and pad the clip. This will help to prevent your mast from breaking if you put your weight on it when falling.

Universal joint and mast track

A correctly fitted, rubber-mounted mast foot fitting requires no maintenance but make sure that the mast can rotate freely above the universal joint. The joint should therefore incorporate low-friction washers.

If you notice cracks in the rubber of your mast foot or if the metal plate at the end is coming loose from the rubber, you should fit a new rubber for your own safety. The self-locking nuts holding the adaptor should be replaced from time to time if they have been undone a great number of times. If you can tighten and undo them without using a spanner then it is time to replace them.

Your wetsuit and shoes

If you pay attention to the care of your wetsuit now and again it will last longer. Keep it out of direct sunlight as far as possible, and rinse it out thoroughly after use. When putting a single-lined wetsuit away for the winter rub it with talcum powder and wash and lubricate the zips with a greaseless lubricant. Keep neoprene wrapped up in polyurethane or cloth. Wetsuits last better if they are hung up when not in use, rather than folded.

The sail

The sail is the only part of your equipment which will wear out. No matter how well you look after your sails in the end you will need to replace them, but with the correct treatment you can greatly prolong their life.

Here are a few hints:

● Always fold or 'flake' the sail in a zig-zag along the leech; leave Mylar sails rolled or very loosely folded
● Do not fold or bend the windows
● Each time you stow your sail make the folds in a slightly different place so that it does not develop permanent creases
● When drying a sail in the wind do not let it flap, and on no account release the outhaul to let it blow as this will severely weaken the coating in the sailcloth and stretch the leech

● When drying the sail always loosen the downhaul
● If you travel with your sail wrapped round the mast on the car roof, you should protect it with a mast bag from dust, dirt and sunlight.
● Do not leave your sail lying in shallow water
● Patch small tears in a sail immediately, otherwise they will tear into large holes; adhesive sail-repair tape will do as a first-aid measure.

The Theory of Sailing

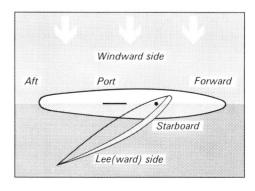

Directions and terminology

Windsurfing has borrowed many terms from boat sailing which do not occur in the everyday vocabulary. Leaving aside the highly esoteric words, many sailing terms are very useful and precise. It is difficult, for example, to orient oneself on the water using 'right' and 'left'. If you say 'there to the right', it depends on the position of the speaker and the listener as to whose right or left. 'There to starboard' always means: on the right-hand side looking towards the bow (or *forward*). *Port* and *starboard* refer to the left and right sides of the board, when looking forward.

If the wind is coming over the port side of the board it is said to be sailing on *port tack*, if over the starboard side it is on *starboard tack*.

Every object has a *leeward* (downwind) and a *windward* (upwind) side in relation to the wind. Anything on the side where the wind is coming from lies *to windward*, similarly anything on the side away from the wind lies *on the lee side* or *to leeward*.

Changing direction

Steering terms always relate to the wind:

Luffing up or *heading up* is turning into the wind. *Bearing off* or *away* is turning the bow away from (off) the wind; sailing more downwind. Also *falling off* the wind.

After every steering movement the sail must be reset to present the best possible surface area and angle of attack to the wind. This is why as soon as we have luffed up we will *pull in* or

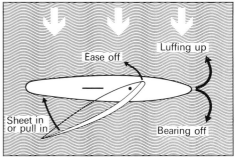

sheet in the sail, i.e. the sail is brought closer in line with the board.

After bearing away we *ease off* the sail: in other words, it will be at a greater angle to the board. As we move the sail we turn the upper part of the body so that the line across the shoulders is either more along the line of the board (hauling in) or more across the board (easing off).

Points of sailing

When sailing and windsurfing there are various ways of deciding which direction to take. You can simply sail where the winds take you, or choose a particular objective or direction.

The different headings in relation to the wind are called the *points of sailing* and have their own names. A course diagonally into the wind is *close-hauled*, or *sailing to windward*.

Sailing across or nearly at right angles to the wind is known as *reaching*. If the wind comes from the side at 90° to your board, it is *on the beam*, and you're *beam reaching*.

Broad reaching is sailing diagonally before the wind, with it coming over the back part of the board, though not directly from astern.

When you are sailing in the same direction as the wind you are said to be *running before the wind*, or sailing *dead downwind*.

If you luff up too far into the wind you will only be able to keep the sail filled by bringing it in so far that the board will begin to move backwards with the wind. The arc where the board *in irons* can no longer sail forwards is called *into the wind*. This will vary according to the type of board but it is approximately 90°, centred on the *head to wind* position.

A sail will always fill to leeward of the board. Therefore a board which has the wind (the wind side or windward)

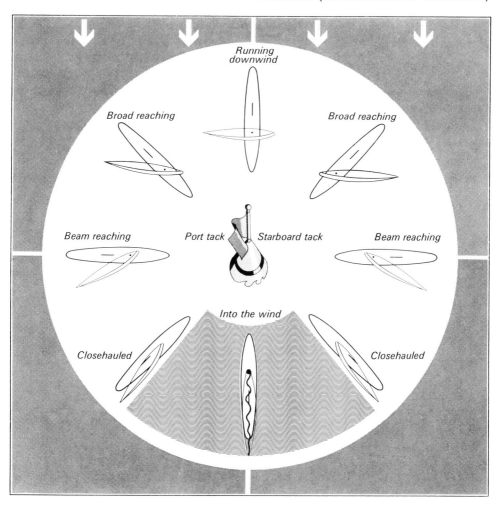

Running downwind

Broad reaching

Broad reaching

Beam reaching

Port tack   Starboard tack

Beam reaching

Into the wind

Closehauled

Closehauled

coming over its right is on the starboard tack and has its sail and boom on the port side. Only when running before the wind can the sailor choose whether he will have the sail on the port or starboard side for the same course. Windward and leeward are behind and in front of the sailboard, respectively, on a downwind *dead run*.

The wind as a motor

Have you ever wondered how it is that you not only sail as primitive craft did with the wind more or less behind, but you can even sail against the wind? Irrespective of which point of sailing you are on, the sail operates in accordance with two quite different principles. When you are sailing with resistance, as you can when the wind is from astern, the sail will act as a brake on the air which constitutes the wind and its force will be passed on to your movement. On the basis of this principle anything can be blown along by the wind, but only in the same direction as it is blowing.

When you are sailing with lift, the cross-section through the sail is the decisive factor that causes the movement. The curvature of a sail deflects the air smoothly from its course producing a condition between the inside and outside of the sail similar to a pressure gradient. This draws the outside of the curved surface diagonally forwards, setting up component forces at all points on the surface of the sail, though we can think of these as acting at one point of force and at approximately 90° to the chord line.

The curve of the sail causes the lift from the wind to act diagonally forward until the boom is approximately over the centre of the board; thereafter it will act across the board, pushing it sideways, then very soon backwards. So you can only sail into the wind until the sail lies along the board.

As long as the wind still comes diagonally from ahead the board will continue to move forwards, but this will diminish in relation to the sideways

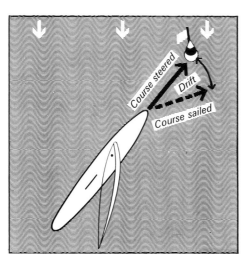

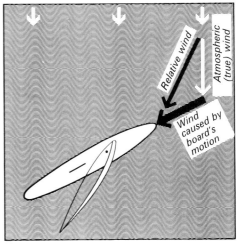

When sailing fast a fully extended daggerboard can lead to a capsize.

force which produces more leeway the closer to the wind you sail. By keeping your sail in the best position you will keep the most favourable balance between forward and transverse forces. If you gradually harden in the sail you will have found this position when the wind stops fluttering the luff.

Although the lateral area of your board provides some resistance to the transverse forces it still does not prevent a certain degree of sideways movement (leeway). The downwind deviation from the course you are steering is called *drift*, and it increases the closer you sail into the wind and the slower you thus move. This is also the cause of capsizes while sailing at speed: the opposing actions of the transverse force on the sail and the

resistance of the board below the fulcrum produces a twisting effect which if strong enough will cause the sailboard to capsize. If your board has this tendency you should increase the size of the fins and daggerboard.

The relative wind

If you look at a number of boards sailing on the same course you will notice that they do not all have their sails trimmed in exactly the same position, and yet it may well be that all of them are correctly trimmed to the wind. The reason for this is that the wind strength and direction can actually vary from one board to the next.

When boards or boats are stationary the conditions affect them all equally; the wind blowing over them is the *true wind*. However, once they start to move a headwind arises from their own motion. You will notice that the wind you feel now appears to be stronger and it is coming more from the front: you must therefore trim your sail to this apparent wind. The direction and strength of the wind 'felt' by the board will change constantly depending on its speed through the water, which affects the wind generated by the board's own motion, and the true wind: the resultant of the two is called the *apparent wind*.

In squally conditions the apparent wind will shift aft, but when the squall drops it will draw ahead again as the board speeds up in the gust.

In strong wind conditions the apparent wind can be troublesome for the windsurfer as he gets onto his board. As soon as he starts to move off the sail pushes him into the water to windward: on account of the rapid acceler-

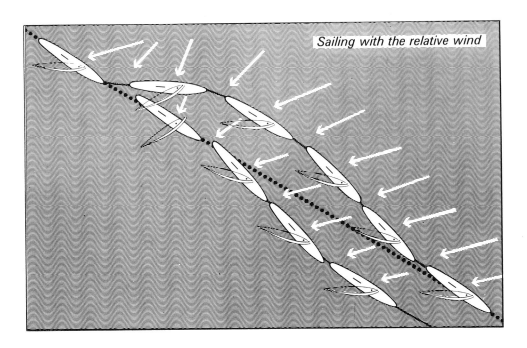

ation in board speed the apparent wind swings sharply towards the bows and if the sail has not been pulled in far enough it will catch it and push it over to windward.

When sailing in waves you should sail along the fronts of the waves with a closehauled sail as they will push you along and you will travel correspondingly faster with the apparent wind stronger and coming forward of the beam.

If you sail along the troughs behind the waves and they cause you to slow down, the apparent wind will shift astern. If you do not ease off the sail enough the airflow over it will separate and you will get a ducking.

Steering the board

Unlike boats, sailboards do not have a separate steering mechanism such as a rudder, but they are steered by chang-

ing the position of the rig to windward and leeward. The force of the wind above the surface of the water and the resistance of the board in the water develop torque which turns it to windward when the rig is to leeward, and vice versa (see diagram).

This effect can also be produced by the angle of the board in the water, as occurs to a marked degree in the case of planing boards without centreboards. In this case the torque is determined by the resistance of the water flowing against the board and its position in relation to its axis. A fully extended daggerboard will take most of the resistance, and due to the fact that when the board is fitted at an angle the daggerboard is pushing out to the opposite side, a board with it down will always turn away from the weighted and lower side. The forces on the dagger produce drag on the board causing it to turn around its axis.

A sailboard without a daggerboard will always turn towards the weighted side as in this case it is the surface of the board as determined by its shape, and the surface area of the fins, which act against the water. Angling the board immerses its inside edge causing it to turn around it; the bottom rocker and profile curvature of the rails also play a part. The torque effect is increased by outside thruster fins.

A board is said to have **lee** or **weather helm** if when in its optimum sailing trim and sail position it has a tendency to veer off to leeward or windward, respectively. The board is sailing in its optimum position when the rig is correctly set to the wind and angled sufficiently far to the stern to close the gap between the foot of the sail and the board.

When the centreboard is angled back it has the same effect as swept-back fins and when the mast is in the forward position the board will have lee helm.

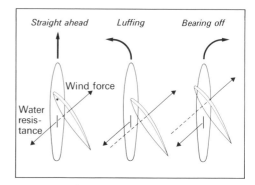

Rescuing a Drowning Person *facing page*

Drowning people instinctively clutch at anything in the water, including their rescuer. Using a board, one is safe from being pulled underwater; once the victim is on the board he will cling to it.

The following method can be used:
—Turn the board bottom up. Pull one of the victim's arms over it until his chest touches.
—Put a knee on the side near you, grip the victim's arm with one hand and the far rail with the other. Turn the board over, pressing down with your knee.
—The victim should end up lying face down with his torso across the board and one arm over it. Lift his legs up, keeping his arms on either side so they can grip. Turn his head sideways.

Signal for help and get the victim ashore quickly for resuscitation.

Rights of Way

Though windsurfing is a sport, you must be aware of the principal rules and do's and dont's applicable where you sail. Ignorance of these can endanger your own safety and be very expensive. Harbour authorities, bye-laws and bodies governing inland waters may all control navigation. The Rules given below are part of the International Collision Regulations which pertain to coastal and open sea waters and are in general very similar to local rules.

Although they may appear to be written for ships and larger pleasure craft, they also apply to windsurfers, who have the same responsibility for not hindering or endangering other craft, proceeding in rights-of-way situations according to the Rules, heeding buoyage and the manoeuvring signals given by other craft, and especially for keeping a good lookout.

Learn the **Sound Signals** that indicate ships' intentions or warnings.
1 short blast: I am altering course to starboard
2 short: I am altering course to port
3 short: my engines are going astern (the ship may not yet be *moving* astern, though).
5 short: Wake up! *or* Look out!

Boards may be prohibited from busy shipping channels and some harbours. And sailing at night or in poor visibility is obviously dangerous.

Pages 90–2 show how the Collision Rules apply in some common situations. The craft having right of way has a duty to 'stand on' and hold her course and the 'give way' craft is obliged to avoid her. However, if you have the right of way and it becomes clear that the other is not going to take avoiding measures, or sufficient measures, it becomes your duty to do so. This is a common problem where pleasure craft mix with shipping or fishing boats: it is better to try to avoid confrontations.

Racing craft are governed by the Collision Rules in relation to boats that are *not* racing, and the latter are not obliged to give them priority just because they are racing. But if you see *any* boats bearing down under spinnakers, or nearing the mark of a course, it is good sense as well as courtesy to keep out of their way.

Important Rules

Fig. 1 *Power driven vessels give way to sailing craft, except when they are fishing or restricted in their ability to manoeuvre, e.g. by shallow water or when towing. Sailing boats using their engines are deemed to be powered craft. Hold a steady course so the 'give way' vessel can see how to avoid you.*

Fig. 2 *Port tack (wind coming over the port side) gives way to starboard tack.*

Fig. 3 *Windward (upwind) craft gives way to the leeward one, when both are sailing and wind is on the same side.*

Fig. 4 *Overtaking craft must keep clear of the overtaken one, until finally past and clear. If the overtaking board were to pass the other on the leeward side, she would still not acquire the right of way because the Rule that 'overtaking craft keep clear' takes precedence over*

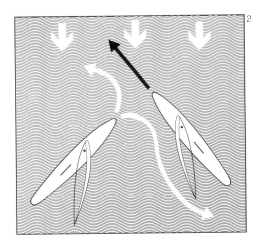

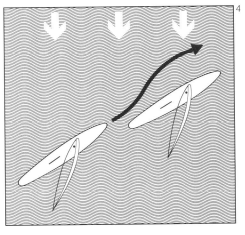

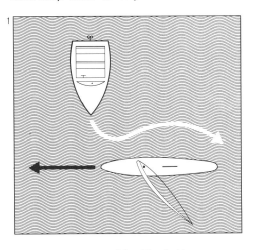

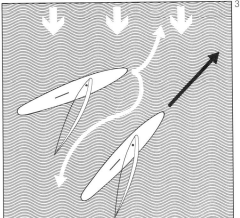

the Rule illustrated by Fig 3. You are overtaking another craft when coming up on them from behind or at an angle of more than 22.5° behind their beam. You must also pass at a safe distance.

'The overtaking craft must keep clear' also applies to jumping. The jumper had to fall off in mid-air to avoid landing on Karl Messmer's board. (page 91).

Yacht and dinghy sailors often cannot tell what boards are capable of doing next, or how quickly. Their larger sails can cut off your wind (as can the sides of ships) and you may not be able to manoeuvre.

Remember that from the bridge of a ship or barge there may be a large 'blind area', especially ahead. Even if you can be seen, their momentum makes last-minute avoidance impossible if you should fall in or lose wind. Also, large craft slide sideways as they turn. Passing well clear and behind is almost always the safest course.

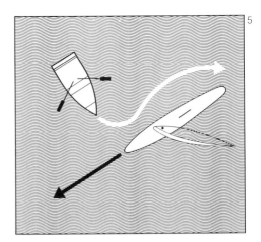

Fig. 5: *Man-powered boats give way to sail*
Fig. 6 *Sail gives way to larger vessels on some inland waterways or where their draft restricts them to a deep-water channel. You must change your heading in good time, not at the last minute, and by a large enough angle to make your intentions clear well before you come near the other vessel. Then hold your new course.*

Illegal and dangerous! ▶

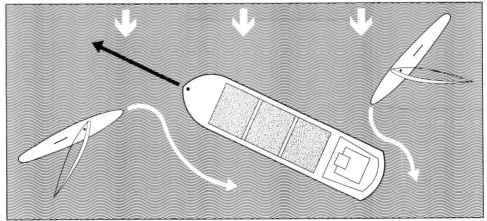

Car-top Board Carrying

You should not generally experience any problems in car-topping your board. However, every country has its own regulations and you must enquire from the police wherever you intend to drive. *The following is only an outline of main points which such regulations usually concern themselves with.*

- There is generally a permitted maximum weight for the roof load, which may depend on the type and weight of vehicle.
- The amount by which the roofrack or its load may project beyond the car's width and length is usually regulated; again, in some cases it relates to the car's size.
- Anything that does extend beyond the car body usually must be marked so as to draw the attention of other drivers and pedestrians: by a red flag or rag in daylight and lights at night. This is to stop other drivers or pedestrians colliding with it, but it will also help you in manoeuvring.
- There may be a permitted maximum all-up weight of vehicle plus load.

Obviously you should only use a strong rack that can be securely attached to the car, with a capacity of at least 50 kg for one board. The best type of attachment is broad straps which should be regularly checked.

On a long journey check the straps about ten minutes after starting off and at least every time you stop. This applies particularly in wet weather and when there is more than one board stacked on top of the other, or if the boom is strapped to the board. If the boom shifts slightly, the board will soon work loose.

As a precaution against theft use a locking roof rack approved by the insurance companies, the feet of which can also be locked to the car. However, you should realize that these are not truly thief-proof. Additional measures to physically secure the board and rig to the car are worthwhile.

If the roof rack is overloaded it will bend the gutter or perhaps its clamp, and may come off.

Secure the board separately from the mast and boom.

Racing

Many windsurfers turn to racing when they get bored with sailing casually up and down. In this way they can compare their ability in direct competition with others.

The point of competing is clearly to win. In order to do so you must often win or do well in a number of races (usually five) which make up the competition. Each placing gives you so many points and the sailor with the lowest number of points is the winner. The table below sets out the point system as used by the IYRU (International Yacht Racing Union). It can be seen that this gives a points bonus to the first six finishers, and particularly to the winner, of each race.

Competitions are normally run according to IYRU rules, which are reguarly reviewed in the year after the Olympic Games.

Courses
On the opposite page you see a triangular course as used in windsurfing championships. A different course is used for Euro-Funboard and World Cup regattas which is better suited to funboards.

The Olympic Point System

Placing	Points
1st Place	0
2nd Place	3
3rd Place	5.7
4th Place	8
5th Place	10
6th Place	11.7
7th and all lower placings	Points according to position + 6

The start
The flying start, taken from boat racing, has the sailor trying to be travelling as fast as possible over the starting line when the starting gun is fired. The line is usually drawn between a buoy and the starter's boat. From this point your course goes to windward to the first mark, then you turn either to port or starboard as directed. Anyone crossing the starting line too early is called back and loses his right of way until he has started correctly. A faulty start may mean disqualification.

Other races may start on shore; this is known as the 'Le Mans' start. The sailors are spread out along a starting line on the shore. When the starting pistol is fired they push their boards into the water and make a beach start. The finishing line is then also on the shore: indeed it may be some way up the beach and require the competitors to run, carrying their boards, to the finish.

Starting procedure
Study the Race Instructions.

Visual signals take precedence over the audible signals, and will be perceived first at any distance.
- Ten minutes before the start the warning/preliminary signal is given together with a course signal and the Class flag is hoisted.
- The preparatory signal goes five minutes before the start and flag **P** (Blue Peter) is hoisted; thereafter the Racing Rules are in force.
- A gun and flag **I** *may* also be used one minute before the start: boards must then keep behind the start line.
- Both flags are lowered when the starting signal itself is given.

You do not need much knowledge of definitions and rules to begin racing. A few of the important and most commonly encountered ones are given here. (The entire text of the IYRU Racing Rules is published as a small book.) However, you will quickly find yourself in situations where the very limited summary here will not be sufficient for you to understand what is happening, or to exploit it by knowing the Rules.

Definitions

Clear ahead, clear astern, overlap. A board lying behind an imaginary line drawn at right angles to the stern of the board in front is lying *clear astern* while the other is *clear ahead*. Once the mast or board behind passes this line an *overlap* exists. Boards overlap when neither is clear as astern; or when, although one is clear astern, an intervening board overlaps both. So, if

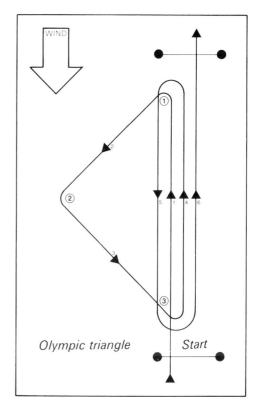

Olympic triangle   Start

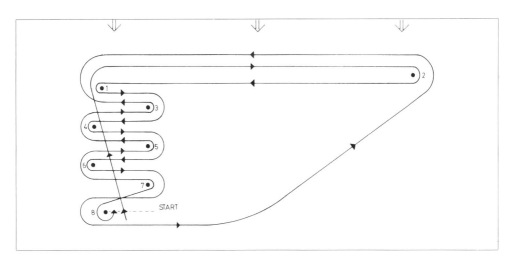

World Cup course. Sailed in the simplest possible way it has two tacks and some fourteen gybes with no dead runs.

Next page: *Start of an Open Class race: the gun is about to go.*

Le Mans start of a surf race

Visual Racing Signals

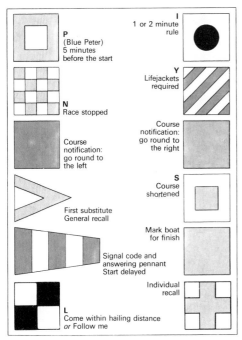

P
(Blue Peter)
5 minutes
before the start

N
Race stopped

Course
notification:
go round to
the left

First substitute
General recall

Signal code and
answering pennant
Start delayed

L
Come within hailing distance
or Follow me

I
1 or 2 minute
rule

Y
Lifejackets
required

Course
notification:
go round to
the right

S
Course
shortened

Mark boat
for finish

Individual
recall

three boards overlap, the hindmost one is also overlapping the leading one.

A *proper course* is any course which a board might sail *after* the starting signal, in the absence of competitors affected, to finish as fast as possible.

Racing Rules

A board to leeward has right of way over a windward board on the same tack. A port tack board gives way to starboard. The overtaking sailor must keep clear of the overtaken one but he can choose which side he wishes to pass on. If a board is overtaken to windward he is allowed to 'luff' the overtaking board, in other words without warning he can round up into the wind as hard as he likes without warning. But once the overtaking sailor comes level with the mast foot of the other board he calls out 'mast abeam' and the overtaken board must drop back onto his proper course.

G65 must expect a protest as when manoeuvering you must keep clear.

G65 has the right of way as he is on the inside. G7 will have to turn 720°.

When several boards are rounding a course mark on different tacks the rule 'port tack gives way to starboard tack' applies, but if two boards are on the same tack then the inside board, closest to the buoy, has right of way if it can overlap the other before coming within two board lengths of the mark.

A board must keep clear of another board which is manoeuvring. A board is regarded as having started to tack from the moment when it is beyond head to wind, and the manoeuvre is considered to have finished when the sail has filled again on the new course.

A gybe is considered to have started when, with the wind aft, the boom has passed the longitudinal centreline of the board, and is completed when the sail has filled on the new tack.

A sailor who has collided with another board may have to pay a penalty by turning his board through 720° at the first opportunity. While doing this he must keep clear of all other competitors.

Racing and other vessels

Competitors in a race do not have any right of way over other craft except as they may have under the Collision Regulations. Even when you are racing you must obey the right of way rules, though it is more sportsmanlike of other sailors to waive their priority and keep out of the way of racing craft. However you should realize that non-windsurfers cannot always tell what courses and manoeuvres are open to boards. Also, they may be restricted by their deeper draft or for other reasons.

Following pages: the Racing Rules still apply. Learn them thoroughly before entering crowded races.

The Natural Environment

The enjoyment of sport is very dependent upon an unpolluted environment. Recreation areas are being subjected to an increasing level of air and water pollution, and we can all be directly affected by the accumulation of rubbish and effluent.

Windsurfers are also open to the charge of disturbing the natural environment and this cannot always be denied. We are all aware that there are people whose enthusiasm for their sport causes them to ignore the interests of nature and the rest of the public, but it is up to everyone to help counter this tendency and do their best to prevent the countryside from being turned into a rubbish heap.

Unspoiled countryside is not only a matter of clean air, water and beaches but it also involves a wealth of animals and plants. Enclosed nature reserves with restricted areas only provide a certain amount of protection, but the very reason for the restriction is to allow the flora and fauna to regenerate and thrive away from invading humans. Lack of consideration for wildlife may well result in even more reserves and prohibited zones, so for the benefit of everyone, observe the few rules we offer.

Observe the Country Code

- Do not destroy any vegetation which is a habitat for wildlife. Keep at least fifty yards away from the following areas which are often haunts and breeding grounds of birds and fish:
  - —reed and withy beds
  - —tree-lined banks and those where plants and undergrowth obscure the shoreline
  - —gravel, earth and mud banks
  - —shallow water, especially if you can see weeds growing in it.
- Keep clear of flocks of birds on the water. Keep at least 500 yards away from mudflats, nesting grounds and other wildlife haunts.
- Find out about the restrictions in your sailing area. There may be certain times of year when sailors are unwelcome near or in nature reserves.
- Certain internationally important wetlands are the habitat of rare animals and plants. Be especially careful if you sail in these areas.
- Use toilet facilities when provided and take your litter home with you.

Dispose of your rubbish: Porto Pollo autumn 1983. A small contribution to environmental pollution.

The island of Sylt in early 1983: a beach start in metre-deep foam resulting from a high phosphate content in the water and heavy surf. A large-scale contribution to environmental pollution.

Tides

The rise and fall of tides is not the same everywhere. Inland seas such as the Mediterranean, the Baltic, the Persian Gulf and the Black Sea have very small tidal rise and fall.

The moon, the earth and the sun exercise a force of attraction on each other. As it is a fluid, water is more easily affected by these forces than the land. Attracted by the pull of the moon, water is drawn to that side of the earth and to the opposite side. This occurs more strongly in large expanses of water such as the oceans. The accumulation of water produces oscillations which reach the shore in the form of high and low tides. The narrow mouth of an inland sea greatly restricts the effect of these tidal movements.

As the earth rotates the moon remains relatively speaking in the same place, so different parts of the earth are turned towards and away from the moon each day. The buildup of the high tide is therefore produced, for example in the North Sea, at intervals of 12 hours and 25 minutes. But as the moon is also rotating round the earth, times of tides in one place are later by approximately 30 minutes, through a 12 hour cycle.

The movement of the moon produces yet another effect, the spring and neap tides. When the moon is in line with the earth and the sun its influence is added to that of the sun so that high tide is higher and low tide lower, i.e. the *range* increases. These *spring tides* last for four days.

When the moon is not in line with the earth and the sun but at a right angle, the sun's effect diminishes the attraction of the moon and during the four days of a *neap tide* high water is relatively low and low water higher.

Between the neap and the spring tides there are three days of mean tides with a medium level of high and low water. Neap tides occur at full and new moons, i.e. about two weeks apart, with springs also two weeks apart alternating between them.

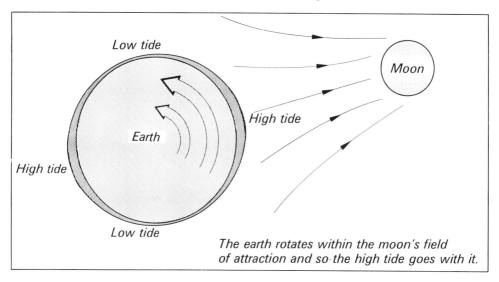

The earth rotates within the moon's field of attraction and so the high tide goes with it.

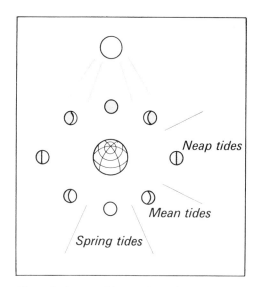

The relative positions of earth, sun and moon produce phases of the moon and change in tidal range.

For sailors, a knowledge of the vertical movements of the tide in their locality as well as the horizontal movements (streams or currents) is necessary. Tides can vary considerably within quite short distances along the coast, and *tide tables* show the times and heights of high and sometimes low water. These are based on predictions made by the hydrographic authorities and actual tides may differ. Weather conditions, especially periods of strong winds, can cause buildups that distort the normal pattern of heights and times, and also the timing and strength of streams. Tide tables often appear in local newspapers, or as cards printed by chandlers and fishing shops, as well as in the fuller but more cumbersome Admiralty Tide Tables and nautical almanacs. The predictions are given for various Principal Ports spaced round

the coast, with corrections for the time and height differences between these and many intermediate places. Local tables are perfectly adequate if you are not travelling round the coast.

Tidal streams

The horizontal tidal movements are obviously important to windsurfers. They can not only be strong enough to affect one's progress but also give rise to such things as overfalls (tumbling, irregular waves where streams cross rough bottom) and tide-rips (where the flow suddenly becomes much faster) which are often dangerous. The stream also changes the shape of waves and even the apparent wind. When tide is flowing against the wind ('wind over tide') waves can be noticeably larger, steeper and more awkward, even for boats, than when

ST HELIER, JERSEY
HIGH & LOW WATER 1985
G.M.T. add 1 hr for Summer Time

MAY				JUNE			
Time h.min.	Ht. m.	Time h.min.	Ht. m.	Time h.min.	Ht. m.	Time h.min.	Ht. m.
1 0304	2.0	**16** 0301	1.6	**1** 0349	2.9	**16** 0433	2.1
0842	10.0	0834	10.6	0934	8.9	1012	9.8
Su 1517	2.5	M 1521	1.9	W 1559	3.4	Th 1655	2.7
2056	9.9	2051	10.6	2150	9.0	2233	9.7
2 0332	2.5	**17** 0343	2.1	**2** 0426	3.3	**17** 0526	2.7
0912	9.4	0919	10.1	1016	8.5	1112	9.2
M 1542	3.0	Tu 1604	2.5	Th 1638	3.8	F 1753	3.2
2128	9.3	2138	9.9	2238	8.5	2336	9.2

Portion of a tidetable showing times and heights of High and Low Water for specific dates. On May 16, a Monday, HW is at 0834 and 2051, LW at 0301 and 1521 at St Helier, a Principal Port. As Spring tides approach the tides rise higher and fall lower, also tidal streams run faster.

both are in the same direction. Anything sailing on the water is also being carried by the stream, and therefore the wind 'felt' by the board is not the same, in angle or strength, as when it is sailing in still water with the same true wind. *Tidal atlases*, or the tabular information shown on Admiralty charts, will not tell you what the effect is on your apparent wind, but they will show the direction of the streams, their strength in various places, and when they change direction. This information is presented in a 'perpetual' form that does not have to be replaced annually, by being related to times of HW at some nearby Principal Port. So again, understanding tide tables becomes necessary even if the rise and fall of tide don't matter much to you.

TIDAL DIFFERENCES ON ST HELIER

PLACE	MHW		MLW	
	Tm. Diff.	Ht. Diff.	Tm. Diff.	Ht. Diff.
	h. min.	m.	h. min.	m.
Channel Islands				
The Casquets ...	+0 22	—	—	—
Alderney (Braye)	+0 45	−4.8S −3.4N	+0 45	−1.0
Guernsey				
St. Peter Port ...	+0 05	−1.7	−0 05	−0.4
Jersey				
St. Helier	0 00	0.0	0 00	0.0
Rozel	−0 09	−0.1	—	0.0
Gorey	−0 05	—		
Les Ecrehoux ...	+0 10	0.0	+0 15	−0.1
Les Minquiers ..	+0 05	+0.6	0 00	0.0
Iles Chausey	−0 15	+1.7	0 00	+0.7

To the times give in the tide table for St Helier for the desired day, add 45 min to find the Mean HW or LW time at Braye; subtract 9 min to get MHW at Rozel. MLW at Rozel is the same time as St Helier.

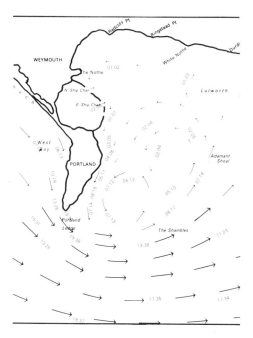

Complex tidal streams shown in an Admiralty Tidal Stream Atlas on the page for 3 hours after HW at Devonport, the nearest Principal Port (which is also 2 hr 40 min before HW at Dover). Larger arrows indicate stronger streams. The figures give normal Neap and Spring rates, e.g. 17,35 means 1.7 knots at Neaps and 3.5 at Springs.

La Torche. Take care! The currents here can run up to speeds of 6 knots.

Wind and Weather

The sun's rays falling on the surface of the earth cause the air to circulate and this is the fundamental effect which produces the weather. When the land has warmed up, this heat radiates back into the surrounding atmosphere producing rising warm air from the earth's surface. Cooler air flows back and we feel this in the form of wind.

Winds

Due to the fact that the rays of the sun are much stronger near the Equator than at the Poles, a continuously circulating airflow system is created. The trade winds which blow from the Canary Isles to the West African coast and across Central America are a part of this circulatory system, as are Pacific trades.

In European latitudes, unfortunately, we do not enjoy such a constant wind and weather system. One of the reasons for this is that we live in a zone where the air circulation is relatively turbulent. Cold air from the Poles and warm air from the Tropics meet in our latitudes. Furthermore, the land gives off more heat into the atmosphere than the water, which causes constantly changing warm and cold currents.

When warm air is rising there will be a drop in pressure near the earth's surface causing a *low pressure area*. The reverse occurs when cold air sinks and a *high pressure area* is produced. As pressure equalization causes air to be sucked into areas of low atmospheric pressure from the highs, winds blow from high pressure zones towards lows. The rotation of the earth produces a circulating airflow which causes these winds to be drawn in a spiral. The greater the pressure difference, the stronger the wind.

On account of the varying circumstances which produce high and low pressure areas in and around Europe, we have a number of characteristic winds: in the South of France, Morocco and the Mediterranean the *sirocco* blows from the south and the *mistral* from the north. The *bora* blows in the Adriatic and the *meltemi* in the Aegean Sea.

The low pressure centres which move across Northern Europe bring about the strong southwesterlies over the British Isles and Continent.

To the north and the south of mountain ranges the *Föhn* occurs. Depending upon the position of the highs and lows air currents flow over the mountains and sweep down onto the valleys as a downslope or catabatic wind which in a Föhn storm can reach Force 8. For other causes there may be very strong, gusty 'waterfalls' of wind over steep cliffs on apparently calm, light-breeze days. These downdrafts are sudden and can knock down large heavy yachts.

Clouds

Cloud, mist and fog are moisture in the air. Vegetation on land and the water at sea release water into the surrounding air. If the air rises very high or when it

Clouds building up into cumulonimbus indicate an approaching cold front. Rain and possibly a thunderstorm on the way.

meets colder air the temperature change cools the moisture-laden air causing the water vapour to combine into tiny droplets or ice crystals, depending upon the temperature. Bright white clouds are formed from the ice crystals while water droplets produce darker clouds. If the drops become too heavy for the updraft, they fall as rain. This occurs particularly in areas of low pressure and thunderstorms.

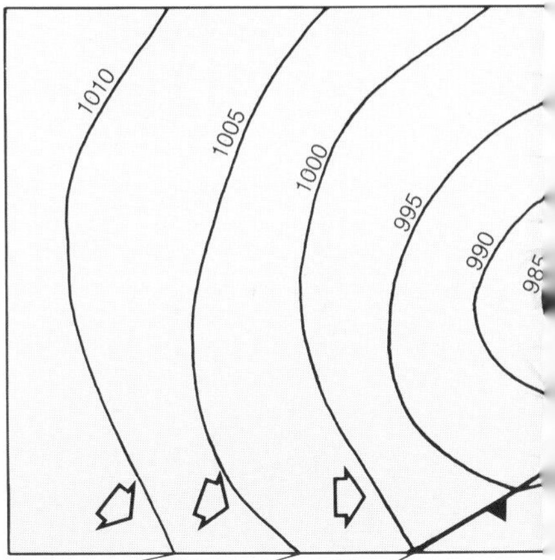

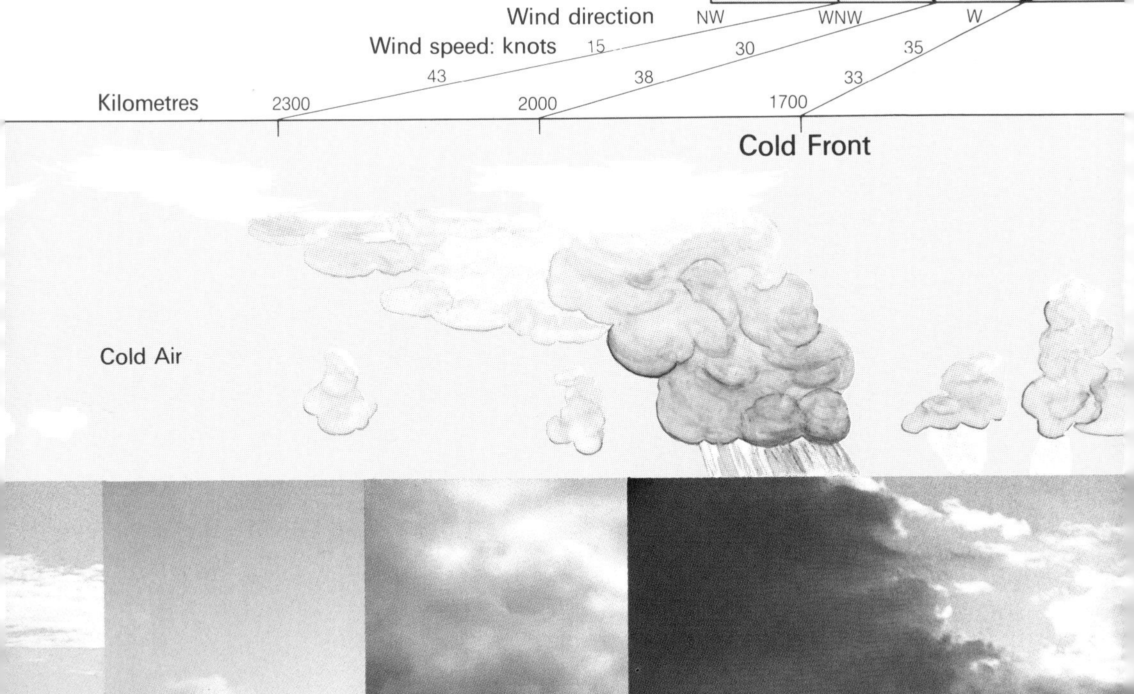

1010 1005 1000 995 990 985

Wind direction	NW		WNW		W
Wind speed: knots	15		30		35
	43	38		33	
Kilometres	2300	2000		1700	

Cold Front

Cold Air

Cumulus and Altostratus

Altostratus

Cumulonimbus

110

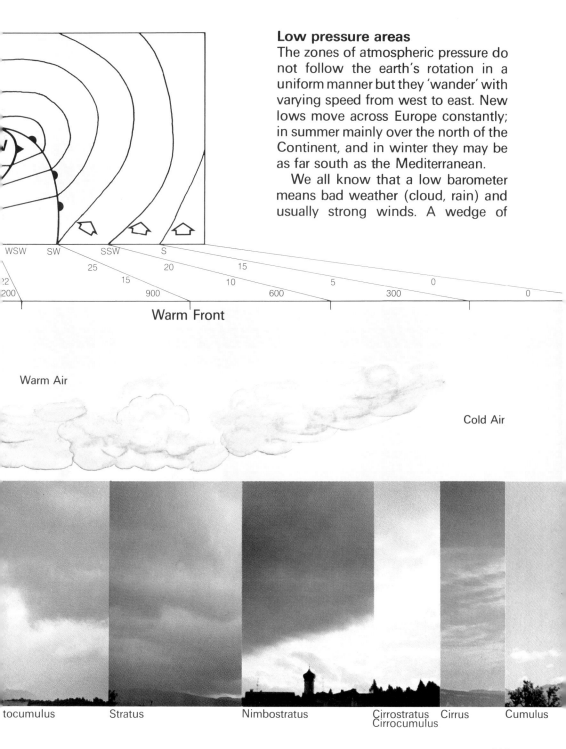

Low pressure areas

The zones of atmospheric pressure do not follow the earth's rotation in a uniform manner but they 'wander' with varying speed from west to east. New lows move across Europe constantly; in summer mainly over the north of the Continent, and in winter they may be as far south as the Mediterranean.

We all know that a low barometer means bad weather (cloud, rain) and usually strong winds. A wedge of

WSW   SW   SSW   S

25   20   15

22   15   10   5   0

200   900   600   300   0

Warm Front

Warm Air

Cold Air

tocumulus   Stratus   Nimbostratus   Cirrostratus   Cirrus   Cumulus
                                        Cirrocumulus

111

warm air is drawn up into the cold air of a low, it cools down on its fronts causing precipitation and changes in pressure and temperature.

When a low moves across a *warm front* is formed on the eastern side of the warm air wedge. This may be heralded by fine feathery cirrus clouds, followed by cirrocumulus, the regular layers of the 'mackerel sky'. The sky gets greyer and greyer as deep layers of altostratus gather and a fine rain soon follows. If the moon is up it will appear veiled behind the early stages of this cloud formation, and when it wears a halo bad weather can be expected in the next few days. When the warm front has passed the cloud cover may break up until the *cold front* comes, bringing with it large formations of cumulonimbus clouds with heavy rain and possibly thunder and hailstorms. Air pressure usually rises sharply before the arrival of a cold front but as the front passes the barometer drops again rapidly. These differences in atmospheric pressure give rise to sudden storms. If a high is following behind a low the pressure will rise slowly and steadily. In late autumn, winter and early spring there are always a number of very low lows, bringing severe gales which affect the whole of the British Isles and NW Europe.

Weather maps and other information

Forecasting the weather is not always easy; low pressure areas move more slowly or even become stationary as they get full. One front can overtake or occlude another or produce an offshoot. Lows take different paths and draw high pressure from different directions. Meteorologists record their observations on weather maps which

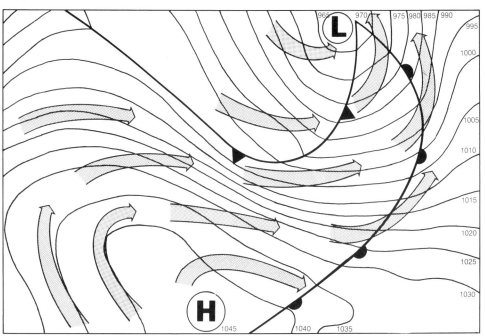

indicate the fronts; isobars are lines indicating all areas of equal pressure. Reports from weather stations are included with data on wind strengths and direction, temperatures and cloud cover. These maps are a major tool in preparing forecasts, though the process is now highly technical. The closer together the isobars the greater the pressure drop and consequently the stronger the wind. Its likely direction can also be seen from the isobars as it blows at about 15° to them.

Weather and gale warnings and reports are broadcast and can also be obtained by phone from Coastguards, etc. Most large areas of inland water

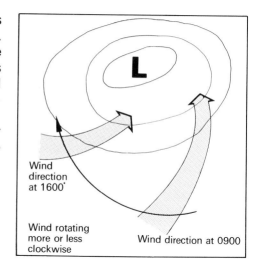

Wind direction at 1600°

Wind rotating more or less clockwise

Wind direction at 0900

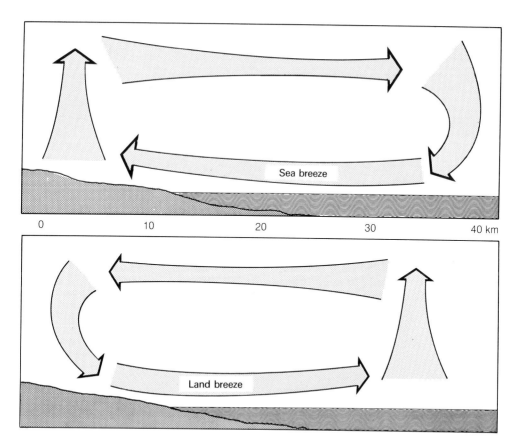

Sea breeze

0   10   20   30   40 km

Land breeze

also have such services to indicate the danger of strong winds and give the wind direction. At the southern end of a low the wind will *veer* (turn clockwise) from SE to SW. If a wind swings from NW to SW, it is *backing* or turning anticlockwise.

Storm signals (UK) for gales in progress or expected are: a black cone hoisted either point up (wind from N of E–W line) *or* point down (from S of E–W line). Continental storm cones are different; there is also a black ball warning of Force 6–7.

Everyone who takes part in water sports must be responsible for finding out about the available weather warnings.

High pressure system

A high pressure area will produce stable weather conditions with a lot of sunshine and gentle 'variable' breezes from different directions. The air will be heated to varying degrees and its rise and fall creates *thermal winds* and *onshore* and *offshore breezes*. Thermals occur particularly in mountainous areas where the slopes reflect more heat than the surrounding plains. The funnel effect of narrow mountain valleys can produce thermal winds up to Force 6 over mountain lakes.

On sea coasts warm air rising over the land draws cool air with it from the sea, giving us our daytime sea breezes. Quite early in the evening this effect will be reversed and the nighttime land or offshore breeze will start. If you have not found out the time when this changeover occurs where you are sailing, you must return to the shore in good time so as not to be caught out by the land breeze. This thermal circulation can be felt as much as 16 miles (30 km) out to sea.

Low cloud ceilings prevent the warm air from rising, inhibiting thermal circulation. This condition, which often occurs in windless conditions, is called temperature inversion. In summer inversions will often produce *heat thunderstorms*. The build-up of warm air breaks through the cloud layer and rises to a great height forming into clouds. A mushroom-shaped storm cloud will discharge its energy in the form of thunder and lightning, releasing its moisture in the form of hail or rain. Force 8 winds are not unusual round the edge of such storms. Because light travels faster than sound you can judge how far away a thunderstorm is by the interval between the thunder and the lightning. If the thunder is heard 3 seconds after you see the lightning the storm is already 1 km away; if the interval is 6 seconds the distance will be twice as far. If you are windsurfing and you hear a thunderstorm approaching turn back to land immediately, even if it means paddling. If you should be caught out in a thunderstorm crouch down on your board and drop the rig in the water to avoid its attracting lightning.

The Beaufort Scale

Bft	kn	km/h	m/sec	m.p.h.	Description	Appearance of the sea
0	–	–	–	–	Calm	Sea like a mirror
1	1–3	1–5	0,3–1,5	1–3	Light air	Ripples form
2	4–6	6–11	1,6–3,3	4–7	Light breeze	Small wavelets
3	7–10	12–19	3,4–5,4	8–12	Gentle breeze	Large wavelets, crests begin to break
4	11–16	20–28	5,5–8,0	13–18	Moderate	Small waves becoming longer, white horses
5	17–21	29–38	8,1–10,7	19–24	Fresh	Moderate waves of longer form, many white horses
6	22–27	39–49	10,8–13,8	25–31	Strong	Large waves forming, white foam crests, spray
7	28–33	50–61	13,9–17,1	32–8	Moderate gale	Sea heaps up, foam in streaks on water
8	34–40	62–74	17,2–20,7	39–46	Fresh gale	Moderately high waves, edges of crests breaking
9	41–47	75–88	20,8–24,4	47–54	Strong gale	High waves, crests topple and roll over. Dense streaks of foam, poor visibility.
10	48–55	89–102	24,5–28,3	55–63	Storm	Very high waves, long overhanging crests. Dense white foam streaks.
11	56–63	103–117	28,4–33,5	64–73	Violent storm	Exceptionally high waves. Sea covered in foam patches.
12	64 and over	over 117	over 33,5	over 74	Hurricane	Air filled with foam and spray, sea white. Bad visibility.

It is a pity if the life of a sail is shortened by careless treatment. Your sail will last longer if handled properly. If you bear the following points in mind your sails will give you many hours of wear and pleasure.

Storing the Sail

The best way of keeping sails is to always put them back in the sailbag or protective cover supplied when you bought them. If you wrap it round the mast you will need a suitable mast bag. Your sail will not last so well if it is always exposed to wind, sun or rain, so always put it away when not in use.

After unrigging your board the sail should be folded up. Make sure that the windows are not folded or after a time you will find you have creases which, especially in low temperatures, will turn into cracks and holes. If this has already occurred stick transparent plastic tape on both sides to prevent its splitting any further.

The question always arises when folding a sail as to whether one should keep to the folds it had when it was new. The advice of the sailmaker is not to always fold a sail in the same place, as you are likely to damage the finish and produce creases which will remain in the sail even in the wind. It is therefore better in principle to have several ways of folding rather than one.

You can clearly roll up a sail made of Mylar or a hard-finish woven sailcloth, and this is often a better way of keeping it, but as already mentioned you will then need a waterproof sailbag to put over it unless you always keep your sail in a dry dark place. If you keep your sail rolled up on the mast make sure that it is loosened off everywhere before you put it away. A sail which is kept taut, especially if still wet, is liable to develop a crease just behind the mast sleeve. This will stretch more and more.

Sails are often folded up damp and packed into the back of a car. If you do this try to make sure that the car is not exposed to strong sunshine as the heat can cause the luff and the luff strip to shrink and is also likely to produce clouding of the plastic window. These effects will partially disappear when the sail is dampened again, but in the long run damp heat will not do your sail any good.

The right way to fold and roll a sail

Keep your expensive sails out of strong sunlight as much as possible. Sails made of synthetics such as Terylene, Dacron or Mylar are particularly sensitive to sun. If you roll up your sail immediately on coming ashore and leave it exposed on the top of the car for long journeys, or if you leave it in a rack in the open air for long periods, the ultraviolet radiation from the sun will cause the sailcloth to age rapidly. If you leave your sail on the rig for months, or even weeks, at a time in a sunny spot on shore the ultraviolet will rot the stitching: it will weaken and the seams and eyelets will start to break under strain. North and Hood Sails have a solution to this problem in the form of a 'seam protection' sealant which comes in a bottle and protects the vunerable stitching, though it does not protect the rest of the sail. Coloured sailcloth is more vulnerable to UV than white.

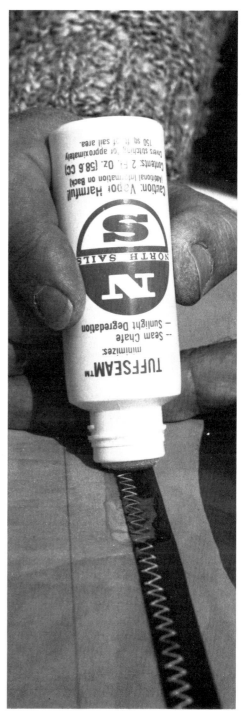

Protection for the stitching

Cleaning your Sail

If you want to ruin your sail, put it in the washing machine!

Dirty marks on the surface of a sail can be removed by rinsing off with fresh water (not sea water). Use a gentle soap or mild detergent and water at blood heat. You can also try careful brushing or rubbing with a soft sponge but always finish by rinsing with clean fresh water.

So be warned and do not put your sail through the washing machine, spin-drier or dry cleaner or you will age it by a whole season. 'So how,' you may ask, 'am I supposed to remove oil and grease marks?' This is difficult even for a professional sailmaker as you can only clean the surface of a sail. Do not on any account use Chlorox or any other bleach as these substances are too strong. Trichlorethylene can usually help and is available at any chemist. Place a sheet of plastic under the sail and rub the mark with cottonwool or a cloth. If it does not disappear completely you will just have to put up with it. To remove blood-stains, first soak and then wash in cold water.

Sails blowing and flapping

If a sail flaps, blows or flogs hard it will wear out more quickly. Make sure your sail is tight when drying: the leech should be sufficiently tensioned to prevent the sail from blowing and flapping. It is very bad practice to leave the sail blowing free from the mast for hours to dry. If a sail left like this has battens they will soon wear a hole in the ends of the pockets and before long your sail will be on its way back to the sailmaker for repair. So we repeat, when drying keep it tight.

Further DIY hints

If the battens are too long they should be cut to fit, filed smooth and have the corners rounded. If the top of the mast pushes its way through the sleeve at the head of the sail, if you tear an eyelet at the clew or if the tack frays, let a professional sailmaker do the repair job for you. If this is impossible at the time you can carry out 'first aid' on the sail. You will need a strong cobbler's or saddler's needle to get through the reinforcing strips at the corners of the

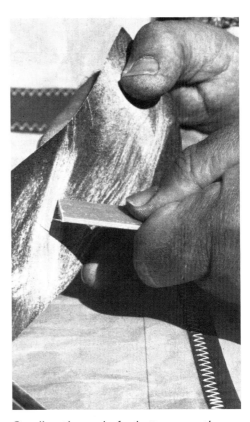

Sanding the end of a batten smooth

sail. Rub the thread in wax (bees wax or candle wax) before starting the job. Unwaxed thread will very quickly dry out and perish. Hard wax is the easiest to use though thread soaked in wax will do. Sew using cross-stitch at a distance of about 6 or 5 mm. The best way to avoid breaking the needle is to push the point through using a sailmaker's palm, then pull the needle with pliers from the other side. If you try to force the needle through the reinforced material not only is it very hard work but you will probably break the needle.

If you should lose a cringle (eye) at the tack or clew you can sew a webbing strap or even a piece of line onto the sail which will act as an eye. Make sure you sew the rope on both sides, as shown, to form a loop and with the stitches passing through all the layers of sailcloth. The corners of sails are especially subject to strain and wear, and such a repair is only a very temporary measure. Take the sail to a professional sailmaker as soon as possible.

Perfect your sailing with...

WINDSURFING TECHNIQUE
Niko Stickl and Michael Garff

A unique approach, using photomontage and sequence pictures, with plenty of spectacular colour shots of world-class sailors in action. Starting from the basic stance and manoeuvres, and with detailed analysis and instruction taking you up to advanced sailing techniques, this is *the* book for improving your performance. Hardback, 180 pages

WINDSURFING RACING TECHNIQUE
Philip Pudenz and Karl Messmer

Two of the world's top sailors analyse, explain and demonstrate the techniques needed for race winning – fast tacking and gybing, speed, mark rounding, 720° turns, trapezing, sail/board trim, starts, tactics and picking the best courses.

Racing courses, signals, scoring, protests and the racing rules particular to windsurfing are all covered, so getting started in racing, or improving your results, are made easier.

Dozens of colour and black/white photos and sequences by Michael Garff make this a unique book.

Hardback, 180 pages

101 FREESTYLE WINDSURFING TRICKS
Sigi Hofmann

Starting with preparatory exercises, and using series photography and a breakdown of each trick into its component moves, this book makes it possible to begin with the easier ones and work up to the most daring and spectacular. The stunts here are graded according to difficulty and wind strength, and arranged in,a logical sequence so that you build on the techniques already learned.

With many good tips on competition and building a freestyle programme, by one of the top international sailors.

Paperback, 120 pages

SAILBOARDS CUSTOM-MADE
Hans Fichtner and Michael Garff

Do-it-yourself sailboard building is a practical, economical way of having a 'fun board', for the kids to learn on, or to try out your own ideas. Hans Fichtner is a shaper for Mistral and here describes the methods and tools that are most suitable for amateur builders and will give a satisfying, quality result.

8 pages of colour board graphics.

Paperback, 120 pages

HEAVY WEATHER WINDSURFING
On Funboards and Sinkers
Jürgen Hönscheid and Ken Winner

Top international sailors explain and demonstrate how to handle strong winds, high waves and surf. The many excellent colour and monochrome action photos and detailed text cover every aspect of funboard and sinker sailing, equipment and tuning. Strong-wind sailing demands a far wider knowledge of wave and wind conditions, safety in breakers, and advanced technique. These are all covered, as well as including how to master carved turns, fast gybing and tacking, sinker sailing, jumping and wave-riding. The sections on competition are particularly thorough and cover surf courses, slalom, and the winning sailing techniques, strategy and tactics for every leg of triangular course racing.
Hardback, 120 pages

WINDSURFING RACE TACTICS
Noel Swanson

A forthcoming title in the Stanford Maritime windsurfing list.

A very comprehensive, fully illustrated analysis of all the various board-against-board situations that occur in racing. The tactical problems of starts, upwind legs, mark rounding, reaching and downwind legs, and finishing are all analysed, along with the relevant Racing Rules, and the best possible courses and manoeuvres that are allowed. There is also advice on broader strategy for pre-start manoeuvres, the different legs of a course, changes in wind and tide, and on the physical and mental preparation for racing.

STANFORD MARITIME
Member Company of the George Philip Group
12 Long Acre, London WC2E 9LP, U.K.

Top flight windsurfing: the Donkey Kick